HOME
NESTING
BASICS

Pat Ross

HOME
NESTING
BASICS

*12 Simple Steps to Creating
a Space That's Truly Yours*

Watercolor drawings by Pat Lattrella

6th
avenue
books

AOL Time Warner Book Group
An AOL Time Warner Company

First Printing: April 2003

6th Avenue Books™ is an imprint of AOL Time Warner Book Group
An AOL Time Warner Company
1271 Avenue of the Americas
New York, NY 10020

6th avenue books™

10 9 8 7 6 5 4 3 2 1

ISBN: 1-931722-26-9
Manufactured in the United States
Book Design by Mada Design, Inc.

Contents

HOME
NESTING
BASICS

From My Home
to Yours

When I decorated my very first "real" home—a spacious one-bedroom apartment in New York City—I made every mistake in the book. With the loose change of a recent raise burning a hole in my pocket, I began to decorate with styles that other people considered chic.

When confronted with a long wall of windows, I covered the expanse with heavy blue draperies, better suited to Versailles. A mile-long sofa looked out of proportion to the rest of the room, but it had come with a pedigree. Since I'd developed no look of my own, I fell for the latest trends, including a lime green shag rug, its pile long enough to hide Easter eggs. A "rug rake," recommended to keep the rug fluffed up, was stored in a hall closet, along with my sense of style and what really made me feel comfortable.

In *Home Nesting Basics*, I'd like to pass along all the things I wish I'd known back then.

"Nesting" is such a nice concept for the way we surround ourselves with the warmth, comfort, and the many aesthetic pleasures of our home place. More than ever, we've come to appreciate the so-called creature comforts as well as the numerous possessions that make up our private sanctuaries. If you've ever watched birds building a nest from scratch in a protected place, you know how hard they work at it. Twig by twig, string by string, their nest evolves. There's a sense of stability when people can make needed and satisfying changes within their homes, rather than starting over in a new place.

The dilemma arises when we have the desire for better nesting, but don't know how to make an impersonal space into a comfortable home, one in which we truly look forward to spending time. It doesn't soothe us to know that decorating decisions can make anyone's head spin. Whether the project is furnishing and accessorizing an empty space from scratch or just replacing that sad threadbare sofa, we need to find our own ways to develop a style all our own, and then cut through the intimidating details to make it ours.

I created *Home Nesting Basics* to guide, solve, and reassure. Why feel trapped in a maze of decorating overload, when a commonsense step-by-step plan answers the familiar home decorating cries:

"Where do I start?"

"How do I fix it?"

"How do I make it mine?"

In plain language, *Home Nesting Basics* provides tried-and-true advice for getting things done quickly, effectively, and on budget. Becoming comfortable with interior design terms, methods, and principles makes it far easier to turn nesting frustrations into challenges, and makes nesting into something we look forward to doing.

Home decorators are as different as the styles they choose, and not everyone has the time or need to use a book as a kind of crash course. For that reason, *Home Nesting Basics* is meant to double as a friendly and well-grounded sourcebook to consult for a range of home decorating dilemmas. First-time home decorators and empty nesters alike come to appreciate that the most successful rooms don't just happen like a magic trick. Personal style is something that evolves over time. With every new project comes a new set of concerns. The basic questions don't go out of date with a new home-fashions trend, and neither do the tried-and-true solutions.

Decorating can become a roller-coaster ride at any given time, for people working on their own as well as those decorating with an involved partner. Since there's no substitute for the right decorating attitude, *Home Nesting Basics* provides time to reflect on more than the right wall color. Lighthearted questions help pinpoint emotional tight corners and blocks, such as dealing with "too much stuff," the inevitable budget, and trying something new. There's a playful list of thoughtful ways that partners working together can add a vital intangible—an open-minded atmosphere—to the decorating equation.

The more I delved into the timeless concepts underlying successful interior design—essentials such as balance, harmony, and color—the more I began to see my own home decorating dilemmas and their possible solutions more clearly. Soon I was inspired to fix all the things that had never quite "worked." With even the smallest

Please keep off the Rug

victory (replacing an outdated lampshade), I'd step back and say to myself, "Now, why didn't I think of that before?" Once I'd seen the light, there was no turning back. I filled an empty corner with a palm tree, rearranged the entire bedroom, and started on a plan to warm up a guest bedroom. When I decided to set off objects in a bookcase by painting the back a pleasing shade of peach, I rediscovered how much simple touches of color—good ol' paint—and sweat labor can effect dramatic change. My hope is that readers will be inspired, also, to enjoy the changes that better nesting can bring.

For almost a decade my passion for American crafts and folk art inspired me to own a popular trend-setting Madison Avenue shop, Sweet Nellie, that specialized in handcrafted decorative accessories and country pieces. The style was comfortable and joyfully eclectic—a look to come home to.

On the Eastern Shore of Maryland, where I was raised, the 4-H Club was an essential part of living in the country. Today, when I look back, I wonder if I haven't carried the club's motto of "Learn by Doing" into my design career. The things I know about the world of design are uncertified by an official card or a diploma in interior design. I've acquired my qualifications by reading, observing, asking questions, experimenting, and making plenty of mistakes. Sometimes, that's enough.

While I was creating the forerunner to this book—an on-line course that ran on the Barnes & Noble Web site—I was in the midst of a major move into a totally redesigned and updated Virginia farmhouse. The higher my stack of floor plans, budgets, paint charts, and pillow choices became, the more new decorating tricks I learned. If this book is more helpfully hands-on than others, it's thanks to a country childhood and an excess of decorating stress in my present life.

The work on the farmhouse was lightened by the support of my design-conscious partner, Ken McGraw, who became my husband while I was writing this book.

A New Sofa
Is Not
Step Number One

Formal   Casual   Contemporary

"When it comes to decorating my home, I never get it quite right." Does this sound like something you might utter, perhaps when the trendy kitchen wallpaper starts to get on your nerves after only a week? If so, relax. This decorating lament is a common one.

You page through all sorts of magazines, clipping pictures of gorgeous rooms. You decide that's the look you want. You hurry out to buy the very same sofa . . . before measuring the wall. When the sofa's delivered, the only space where it fits is in the garage. Does this sound at all familiar?

Decorating your own place can be trickier than getting paint to dry on a rainy day. But take heart. You *can* be your own best decorator, perhaps more successfully than you ever imagined. It doesn't matter if you don't know a sham from a bolster, a paintbrush from a pastry brush; *Home Nesting Basics* starts at the beginning. It arms you with the nitty-gritty to get the job done quickly and smartly. And it takes into account one neglected aspect of design: the right attitude.

Practical and Necessary Goals

Learning from scratch? Know enough to be dangerous? Wonder if you're doing things the right and the easiest way? Although it may sound daunting at first, successful home decorating is a logical *process,* with steps that take you from "armoire" to "zebra skin."

In this book of basics, you'll learn to:

- Discover a personal style with ease
- Communicate your needs, using proper decorating terms
- Take an inventory
- Take measurements and draw floor plans
- Make a budget
- Apply the VIP design principles of space, line, weight, focal point, scale, and balance
- Create an expressive background with color, texture, pattern, and shape
- Learn the best tricks of the trade
- Create a step-by-step plan
- Take pleasure in the many aesthetic aspects of better home nesting (listed last, but way up there in importance)

Getting Emotional

Before you pick up a paintbrush or buy a single lamp, look over a few of the positive *emotional goals* of this book.

- **Trust yourself.** You know more than you think you do. The color of a room or the feel of a fabric affects you. Certain possessions make you smile each time you pass them. The things you choose to live with have tangible and *intangible* value. Your heart tells you when you've made the change from *house* to *home.*

- **Enjoy expressing your sense of style.** Accept your preferences. I love patterned rugs and rarely decorate with anything in the rust orange family. A well-known magazine editor has a passion for anything embellished with shells. Your own style makes a difference between a well-arranged space and a room with soul.

- **Commit to a smart and organized plan for success.** Poorly organized decorating projects are at risk of falling apart. Being careful involves keeping track of papers, writing things down for easy and accurate reference, keeping reminders of things to do.

- **Keep it simple.** Your home will look more tied-together when you take one step at a time.

- **Be patient.** Some of the technical information may seem a bit tricky at first. The reward is more informed choices. I recommend terrific sources at every step of the way and list my favorites at the end of this book.

- **Know when to compromise on design issues.** It's the only way to work with a partner (or child) who shares your space but not necessarily your taste. There's a way to make everyone happy, if you know how to approach the potential quicksand of duo (or trio) decorating.

- **Break out.** Today's more relaxed rules include mixing and matching, leaving windows unadorned, or (horrors!) placing a sofa on a diagonal.

One Point of View

My favorite rooms are a mix and match of shape, color, pattern, texture, and style. My personal style preference is somewhat eclectic—a relaxed combination that includes historic and contemporary elements. In my own home, I like the dramatic style contrast of a favorite ultramodern vase on the Queen Anne–style dining table. In the living room, a modern color-field painting creates a bold background for a camelback love seat. I prefer to let a space unfold with time, adding elements according to what I adore, rather than settling for an item to fill a space. In a home, "instant" is better suited to cake mixes than elements of design.

Over the years, I've come to call this comfortable, yet elegant style "formal country," which is also the title of one of my books.

- **Appreciate your space and what you can do with it.** Find joy in exploring color, texture, pattern, line, shape, balance, and harmony. Use light sources—the natural and the artificial ones—in your home to dramatic advantage.
- **Accept that you'll make a few mistakes.** You'll be able to fix most of them, as well as learn from them. I painted a bedroom the very same sophisticated shade of sleek gray that I'd fallen for in a magazine. In my home, the same color looked cold and drab, and more like a hospital room. Luckily, it took only one coat of a more purple gray to warm up the space.
- **Be realistic about spending within your means.** You can choose a heavenly solid paint color now, and bring in the costly decorative faux painter at a later date.
- **Take the time you need.** Decorating decisions take time, so don't rush the necessary schedule. Enjoy the process!

A Professional's Smart Start

Susan Lyle, a partner in the successful New York City design firm of Hutchings-Lyle, begins any decorator-client relationship by asking a few insightful questions.

- **What is your daily routine and when do you use the different rooms in your home?** Consider the activities of the people sharing your home and the planned use of the rooms. Look around. Where are phones and TVs? Stereos and computers? From her experience over the years, Susan Lyle says this question gives her the best clue as to where people really live. This type of evaluation affects everything from seating to a choice of fabrics. For example, a room used only on special occasions, such as a formal dining room or guest room, has far different lighting requirements than a busy kid-friendly recreational space.
- **Do you entertain? If so, what is your entertaining style—an informal dinner for four or large and lavish buffets? Birthday parties for kids or casual dinners with friends?** The more guests and visitors, the more you'll need to look at your use of floor space. For example, is there an easy flow from one room to the next for a crowd? Do you dine formally? Often? Do you make the same New Year's resolution year after year about inviting more guests more often for sit-down dinners? Don't base your answers on unrealistic aspirations but, rather, on the life you actually lead.
- **Do family and friends frequently come for weekend visits or longer?** The more visitors you

Even small touches in tucked-away areas, *such as a well-organized pantry, turn workday spaces into inviting places. The vintage glass canisters, set next to a canning jar of dried flower stems (left), provide useful storage while also adding interest. The plain metal caps of simple mason jars (above) have been replaced by something livelier.*

have, the more their comfort and space needs come into play. If your sister visits often, consider her favorite color for the guest bedroom.

- **Are you a collector who likes to see every decorative plate on the wall, or someone who prefers stuff to be put away?** The need to plan ahead for things such as wall units and surface space (shelves and tabletops) may be determined largely by personal passions and hobbies.

- **What are the particular requirements for the bedroom?** Assess the proper size of the bed, the selection of decorative pillows (a harem-style pile or the basic pillows for sleeping?), and how you're going to keep the neighbors in the dark. Sleeping habits, such as keeping a window open, even in the dead of winter, or the need for blackout shades, are logical considerations when it's time to select bed coverings and window treatments.

Spilling the Beans

Does your lifestyle include chips and salsa on the couch? Perhaps you should check out the new techno fabrics. They're spill-proof, durable, very handsome, and available in many colors and designs. Explore the options by visiting the following Web sites:

www.jhanebarnestextiles.com, www.carnegiefabrics.com, www.dtex.com, www.maharam.com, and www.knoll.com.

■ **Where do you store your clothes, personal belongings, linens, etc.?** Do you have adequate space, or will you need to plan for built-ins, look for a larger dresser, or hold a three-day garage sale? If you're short on space, there are many creative solutions, such as giving a decorative chest a storage role for small things like candles, coasters, and cocktail napkins. I store batteries and lightbulbs in a collection of covered baskets. Kids' spaces beg for durable and inexpensive plastic storage containers in fun color combinations.

Consider Your Lifestyle

Recent empty nesters rush to redo their living room in white brocade and silk, while a couple with young children and assorted furry pets gets excited about the latest in techno fabrics.

Are you . . .

■ Seeking a totally new look?

■ Starting out in your very own place?

■ Eager to take every home decorating purchase with you when you move?

■ Hoping to upgrade and revitalize your present space on a tight budget?

■ Ready to splurge on your dream look?

■ Merging styles with a partner?

■ Hoping to freshen up the place, hang a few pictures in the right spots, change the furniture arrangement, and add more accessories?

You may be in a category all your own, but the step-by-step advice in this guidebook is meant for everyone.

Unless you're a purist, *deciding on a personal style probably will be a mix of design influences. However, most people lean toward one of three of the most popular decorating styles, all shown here. Country style (top left) is warm and casual; formal style (top right) is more traditionally elegant; and contemporary style (right) tends to favor clean lines and pared-down good looks.*

Halloween Snoop

During the years when my daughter and her friends went trick-or-treating to other apartments in our building, I was always eager to be the chaperone. I'd crane my neck over witches' hats and push aside little monsters for a peek into my neighbors' apartments. Given the identical layout, every apartment had a totally different look. Erica came home with candy, and I came home with new ideas.

What's Your Style?

Be candid with your replies to the following questions about your personal definition of furnishing styles. There are no correct answers. The purpose is to gain a clear sense of your style preferences.

- Does a formal room filled with fragile glass or family heirlooms make you feel uneasy, or do you long to live with historical pieces?
- Does a knickknack shelf jam-packed with tiny collectibles make you cringe, or do you wish you had one just like it?
- Does a place that's bursting with quirky furniture, such as a chair design that walked right out of *Alice in Wonderland,* send you in search of something more sensible?
- Is the cozy, if somewhat cluttered, lived-in look your thing, or do you like your surroundings cleaner, simpler?
- Is a calming tone-on-tone beige (that is, a mix of shades and tints of beige) or a bells-and-whistles assortment of bright colors right for you?

Of course, you answered every question without blinking. That's because it's easy to express personal interests, recognize possessions that please you, and sense moods that make you comfortable. So hold on to your home nesting feelings, and let them play a big role in your style.

Style Lingo

Categories of design styles have evolved over the years. Even though you needn't feel bound by any of the styles, knowing what they're called will help with communicating tastes and needs to others.

Most styles fall into three major categories:

- **Formal:** Also called traditional or classic.
- **Casual:** Also called country or relaxed.
- **Contemporary:** Also called modern.

A Most Unusual Style

When I found out that Max Pine owned a substantial collection of plastic pencil sharpeners, objects more often cherished by schoolchildren, I imagined this business executive's desk drawers jammed with dozens of ordinary sharpeners, plus an ample supply of sharp pencils. However, when Max invited me to his home, there was not an ordinary pencil sharpener anywhere to be found.

Instead, there were one thousand brightly colored pencil sharpeners, each one taking a playful form.

I spotted food-themed pencil sharpeners: apples, peanuts, cakes, and several Popsicles. Pencil sharpeners came on wheels, a chunky VW sharing space with a stylish 1950 Buick. When I asked Max to play favorites, he pointed to a bright red lobster (how could I have missed it?), which pries open to reveal a crab inside, which doubles as an eraser. It was but one of many finds, collected by Max over twenty-five years.

I couldn't resist asking Max how he came to collect pencil sharpeners, much less include the collection in his stylish home decor. "I like kitsch," Max replied—"kitsch" being a term given to familiar and whimsical objects, often considered a part of popular culture. Fans of kitsch deem certain objects, such as a pickle-shaped salt-and-pepper set or a silver cocktail shaker in the shape of a penguin, memorable blends of form and function. Detractors of kitsch declare that objects such as plastic handbags and dashboard hula girls on springs are simply tasteless. Whatever you may think of kitsch, it manages to make a style statement all its own, and be just plain fun at the same time.

I developed a personal fondness for the vacuum cleaner pencil sharpener, a tank-type with hose and sweeper and an absolute replica of the real thing. The collection, set on glass shelving and seen from all angles, creates a kaleidoscope of vivid colors. In close proximity to Max's mostly modern furniture and artwork, the pencil sharpeners have become a part of a highly original decorating scheme.

Recently, Max donated 850 pencil sharpeners to the Please Touch Museum, a hands-on children's museum in Philadelphia. And what's become of the 150 remaining treasures? Max says a replica of the supersonic Concord, a toaster, a Coca-Cola machine, and a traffic light, among others, have been moved to a spice cabinet in the kitchen.

Certain useful words and phrases tell us even more about style variations, such as:

Rustic: Think of lodgepole pines, twig furniture, and country-style checks.

American country: A love of Americana, folk art, and things patriotic.

Cottage style: A relaxed look used for homes at the beach or in the woods.

Formal country: The elegance of formal mixed with the warmth of country.

Shabby chic: Extra relaxed in its outlook, those loose slipcovers are a giveaway.

Trend-setting: On the edge of what's making design news.

Minimalist: A spare, less-is-more philosophy.

A style may be defined by a regional or country influence, such as:

Southwest style: Think of stucco walls and terra-cotta pottery, Native-American artifacts, and pale desert shades.

English country-style: Think of flowered chintz fabrics, comfy overstuffed furniture, and lots of decorative accessories.

French country-style: Picture painted tiles, flagstone floors, a pitcher of sunny flowers on an old plank table.

Caribbean style: Think of brilliant tropical colors, wicker furniture, venetian blinds, and lots of light.

A style may be strongly influenced by a movement or a period of history, such as:

Arts and Crafts: This design movement (late 1800s to the 1920s) extolled honest construction and clean, simple lines, such as a sharp, geometric rendering of flowers on a bowl, or wooden furniture designed with Shaker-like simplicity and usefulness.

Victorian: Named for the long-reigning queen of England, this style prevailed from 1840 to 1900. Think of massive and elaborately carved furniture, fussy bric-a-brac, detailed engravings, and "crazy" quilts.

Art deco: Dominant in the 1920s and 1930s, this style features streamlined shapes, rounded corners, and strong vertical lines, shown to advantage in etched glass paneling, elegant flute-shaped vases, and smart lacquered furniture, with an emphasis on shiny black.

Art nouveau: A style developed in France and Europe in the late 1800s, characterized by asymmetry and ornate flowing lines. Inspired by nature, art nouveau pieces often feature stylized flowers, leaves, and birds, as well as dreamy women with flowing hair.

A decorating style that adheres closely to its influence is known as "purist," "pure," or "historically accurate." A style that combines a variety of elements is said to be more "eclectic," a "blending" of styles. Don't feel pressured to give your look a label. Most people don't want to live in a purist museum; neither do they want to live in a jumbled theme park. Happily, there are many suitable in-between looks.

Tips of the Trade

Exercise buying restraint, especially on a tight budget. It's easy to get carried away. Go for quality and avoid the overly trendy. Well-constructed old pieces, such as family heirlooms and antiques in original condition, hold a timeless character. Depending on the piece, most have a good resale value, which most new furniture does not.

Start with a Daydream

Do you develop decorator's block when it comes to taking that first style step? Need an idea to get you started? Here are a few icebreakers:

- **Form a mental image of your ideal room.** Jot down a simple description. Is it chic and restrained, or charmingly romantic? Do you see overstuffed furniture and needlepoint throw pillows with fringe and braid? Or the clean lines and fine oak finishes of Arts and Crafts pieces?

- **Think of a place you've visited recently that you loved.** It could be a charming cottage on Nantucket, or an elegant suite decorated in shades of pale yellow at the Ritz-Carlton. Think of how it made you feel. Every time you pass the space you intend to decorate, superimpose your vision on it. Hold on to this *mood sense.* When I hear the theme song from *Out of Africa,* do I long for Robert Redford? No—I just want to find white lace curtains and a vintage floral bedspread like the ones I saw in Karen Blixen's romantic bedroom.

- **Visit a museum and study a painting that appeals to you.** What is it about that painting that makes you buy the poster version for your office? The colors, the shapes, the mood? If you find yourself returning to the Cézanne room, then peaches, pink, and strong blues might be your inner color scheme. Brainstorm with vacation photos or even your postcard collection.

- **Think of places you have been, images that have stayed with you.** At a recent lecture, noted interior designer Vincente Wolf showed a slide from a trip to Burma that showed a striking saffron-robed monk. Both the form and the color had struck him. He asked the audience to think about how such an image might translate into their design preferences. Similar design associations may help you arrive at your ideal style.

- **Start assembling a clipping file of favorite magazine pages.** Find a design element in the room shots—a piece of furniture, a period style, a furniture arrangement—which you'd like for your home.
- **Choose a favorite possession.** A brightly painted vase might be the beginning of the perfect color combination.

A Useful Project: About Form and Function

Make a list of any aspects of your daily life that directly affect how you'll make furnishing decisions. Focusing on these considerations is one of the most important things you can do. The physical requirements of the people who live under one roof, or visit on a regular basis, need special attention. For example, if your partner is tall and substantial, you might consider crossing delicate pieces, such as a set of old Windsor chairs, off your list.

If you share your home with a senior person, or someone who's physically challenged, pay special attention to those limitations. For example, for anyone on crutches, small rugs that may slip or slide are dangerous. Sharp edges and clutter may be hard to maneuver around. Consider every room, keeping an eye out for how *all* the members of your household will function in it.

Having to consider the unique needs of children can mean cutting back on decorative detail, opting for durable home purchases, and hanging things just a bit higher than recommended, at least for a while. Grandparents have the challenge of finding ways to protect their well-earned possessions, such as slipping a washable one-size-fits-all cover on a good velvet sofa while grandchildren visit.

Decorating Dilemmas

THE STYLE SNOB

Q: My new neighbor has a smug attitude about her decorating style. "Traditional is just so stuffy! You really ought to go more modern," she says, as though my plan to buy a classic-style sofa would get me thrown in style prison. Yesterday, she dropped off a magazine clipping of a sofa she claims is "all the rage." How can I politely suggest to my neighbor that she mind her own style?

A: A promotional brochure, one of many useful handouts at my local Calico Corners, shows muslin-upholstered sofas and chairs in three style categories: Classic, Updated Classic, and

Traditional. Seeing similar styles grouped together makes it obvious that style definitions may be as subtle as the shape of the arms or as broad as the size of the cushions. Unfortunately, it's easy to get locked in to a rigid style vocabulary, as well as rigid style choices. In all probability, you're not going to change your neighbor's mind by showing this brochure to her. But just wait till your comfortable new sofa is in place! Your neighbor may be able to see for herself that style choices encompass many good looks and variations.

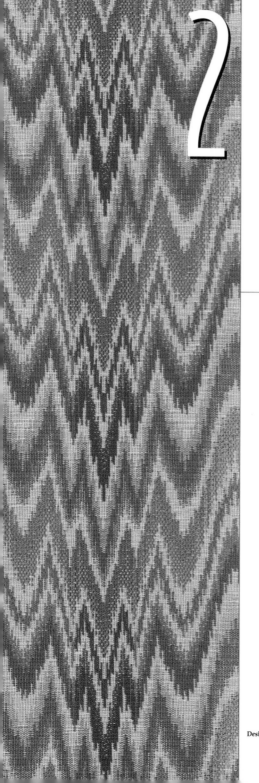

2 QUICK FIXES FOR DECORATING CONFLICTS

Ottoman Conflict

Design from the Laura Ashley Fabric Library™ distributed by Kravet

Few people share the same viewpoint on home style. Loving couples have been known to make a scene in public over which ottoman to buy and how to pay for it. Even the most harmonious decorating situations bring out the child in many of us. That's real life. Unless you're prepared to divide up the rooms, resulting in a fruit compote of design, you need ways to cope with domestic conflicts as trivial as the shade of blue or the right way to hang a picture.

For many years, rarely had I been asked to run as much as a paint sample by anyone for "approval." Recently, I married a design-conscious man who had his own set of designing ideas about every room! Unaccustomed to sharing, at first I balked. Then I discovered that my husband possesses an instinctively fine sense of style, one that complements mine. Our individual styles blend. (At least, most of the time.)

This chapter is about patience, anticipating outcomes, and the gentle art of compromise. It offers tangible ways to take others' tastes and ideas into account when you decorate. By sharing ideas, we expand our own sense of design. Even when a professional decorator comes aboard, suddenly it's the three of you, at least temporarily. While the outcome may be simply terrific, often it's common for one person to feel left out.

The Mars and Venus Decorating Test

Spot the Mars and Venus decorating differences now, rather than later. The following multiple-choice questionnaire is a lighthearted way for decorating partners to brainstorm so that they *remain* partners after the workers have packed their tools and gone home. It's meant to lead to an open-minded discussion.

Choose the answers that best match your gut feelings, no matter how silly they may seem. Ask your partner to do the same, but don't compare answers till the end. Go to the next section to find out how compatible (or not) you are on the design home front.

1. Throw pillows are:
❏ **A.** Essential to the finished look of a room.
❏ **B.** Terrific—the more the merrier.

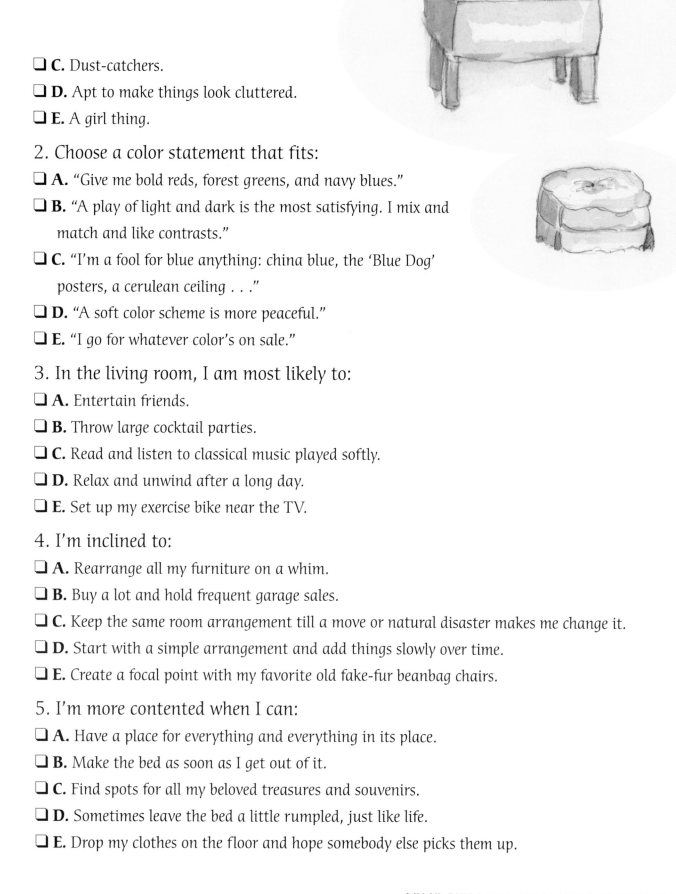

❑ **C.** Dust-catchers.

❑ **D.** Apt to make things look cluttered.

❑ **E.** A girl thing.

2. Choose a color statement that fits:

❑ **A.** "Give me bold reds, forest greens, and navy blues."

❑ **B.** "A play of light and dark is the most satisfying. I mix and match and like contrasts."

❑ **C.** "I'm a fool for blue anything: china blue, the 'Blue Dog' posters, a cerulean ceiling . . ."

❑ **D.** "A soft color scheme is more peaceful."

❑ **E.** "I go for whatever color's on sale."

3. In the living room, I am most likely to:

❑ **A.** Entertain friends.

❑ **B.** Throw large cocktail parties.

❑ **C.** Read and listen to classical music played softly.

❑ **D.** Relax and unwind after a long day.

❑ **E.** Set up my exercise bike near the TV.

4. I'm inclined to:

❑ **A.** Rearrange all my furniture on a whim.

❑ **B.** Buy a lot and hold frequent garage sales.

❑ **C.** Keep the same room arrangement till a move or natural disaster makes me change it.

❑ **D.** Start with a simple arrangement and add things slowly over time.

❑ **E.** Create a focal point with my favorite old fake-fur beanbag chairs.

5. I'm more contented when I can:

❑ **A.** Have a place for everything and everything in its place.

❑ **B.** Make the bed as soon as I get out of it.

❑ **C.** Find spots for all my beloved treasures and souvenirs.

❑ **D.** Sometimes leave the bed a little rumpled, just like life.

❑ **E.** Drop my clothes on the floor and hope somebody else picks them up.

6. The TV set should be:

- ❏ **A.** Hidden inside an attractive armoire.
- ❏ **B.** Concealed under a table by a long tablecloth.
- ❏ **C.** A sleek model in clear view.
- ❏ **D.** A theater-size screen mounted on the wall.
- ❏ **E.** A shrine to football and focal point of the living room.

7. I want my living room to be:

- ❏ **A.** A reflection of my personality.
- ❏ **B.** Elegant but comfortable.
- ❏ **C.** A safe place for my antiques and good things.
- ❏ **D.** The showplace I've always dreamed about.
- ❏ **E.** A reflection of my bank account.

8. If I had to place two pillows on the sofa, I would:

- ❏ **A.** Place two at one end and find a different size and design for the other end.
- ❏ **B.** Casually arrange both pillows near the center of the sofa.
- ❏ **C.** Put one at each end and make sure they match.
- ❏ **D.** Fluff them, karate-chop them at the centers, and make sure no one messes them up.
- ❏ **E.** Pull out all those little "souvenir" airline pillows I managed to stuff into my carry-on bag.

9. You desperately need clothes hangers, so you jot yourself a shopping note that says:

- ❏ **A.** "Assortment cloth-covered hangers."
- ❏ **B.** "Find scented cloth hangers for guest room."
- ❏ **C.** "Inexpensive sturdy plastic hangers. Plenty (red?) for the kids' rooms."
- ❏ **D.** "Wall hooks, pegs, clothing racks, a few hangers."
- ❏ **E.** "See if the cleaner has a bunch of those wire ones lying around."

10. The way you really feel about the decorating taste of your partner(s) is:

- ❏ **A.** "Decorating's more my thing, but I know we'll work it out."
- ❏ **B.** "It may be worth the extra money to have professional decorating help, because neither of us has the time to spend shopping and finding a painter."

❑ **C.** "How do I tell my wonderful bride that I don't share her passion for furniture inspired by *Star Trek*?"

❑ **D.** "We need to discuss our quick-tempered relationship and how we're going to deal with decisions about redoing the family room . . ."

❑ **E.** "I pay the bills, so I get the final word."

How Did You Score?

■ Partners who responded with the same letter answers are on their way to perfect decorating harmony.

■ A's and B's have compatible outlooks, so compromise should be a snap. The same goes for C's and D's.

■ A's and B's see personal style differently from C's and D's, and should be prepared to work out decorating conflicts. The more crossovers, the more potential for standoffs.

■ If both you and your partner came up with a list of straight E's, you're a perfect match for each other.

■ An E paired with an A, B, C, or D is a decorating divorce waiting to happen!

A Design Compromise Solution

Ken has been known to carry wallpaper samples in his briefcase, sandwiched between business documents. He spends lunch hours poking around antique shops and housewares stores. Although his taste tends to be more symmetrical than mine, our style choices rarely become a source of discontent. However, at times when decision-making gets difficult, we turn to a Design Compromise Solution, worked out by us over time. For clarity and harmony, we've devised three possible votes on tricky issues and choices. The votes are short and to the point.

1. "Heads up!"
2. "Just okay."
3. "No way!"

Whether the object in question is a bargain pillow or a substantial armoire, the third vote means that one of us can't bring him- or herself to live with the selection, and so "end of discussion." We save these vetoes for decisions that really matter. The second vote means one of us is not wild about the selection, but can live with it. The first vote makes for a pleasant win-win state of mind. This may not work for every couple or every situation, but it's worked for us.

Comparing Notes

Use your two sets of answers to the Mars and Venus Decorating Test to kick off discussions about areas where you're in sync with a partner, and areas where the two (or more) of you have distinct differences. Start with these topics, but discuss other things that come to mind:

■ Taste in design, color, texture, patterns

■ Importance of order/disorder

He likes the strong straight lines of Stickley. *She prefers furniture with a more curved shape. There's no reason why a compromising couple can't have the best of both worlds by combining their style choices. Here, a bright, sumptuous wing chair shares space with a handsome and ascetic end table.*

- Attention to detail
- Who's really in charge (and whether this matters)
- Three common sources of conflict: TV, window treatments, pillows
- Entertaining preferences
- Compatibility of ideas
- Individual collections, and other personal passions
- Possibility for realistic compromise

Proceed with care if you hit your

A Bear of a Solution

Phil was overjoyed to find a stuffed grizzly bear at a local junk shop. Phil and Jackie's home was filled with tasteful Western artifacts, and the bear seemed like the perfect addition—at least to him. As soon as Jackie saw the bear, she said, "It'll look good in the garage!" After a Western-style standoff, the bear was allowed to stay . . . on the landing of the stairway to the basement game room. Now, when someone heads downstairs, the bear roars—the sound triggered by a concealed pressure switch. Thanks to compromise, the bear's become quite a conversation piece, plus Phil and Jackie can't imagine the stair landing without it.

partner's design hot button. Remember that most home decorators have an irrational shadow side—such as a dislike of traditional brass lighting of any kind (mine); anything with an old peeling-paint finish (his). Now that you've learned a few things about each other, it's time to figure out how to avoid decorating conflicts.

The Knack of Anticipation

The knack of anticipation is an important element in home decorating. In short, you need to look before you leap, alone or together. There are ways to head off colorful partnership conflicts before they begin.

- **Never buy paint from a paint chip.** Paint chips, or samples, are wonderful for exploring the possibilities, but too small to show the full-scale effect. After narrowing down the choices, purchase a small quantity of your choice of paint color and finish, plus the alternate choice, if you're not sure. (You'll read more about this in a later chapter.) With your newly selected paint, cover the preexisting color or finish by painting a three-foot-wide swath along a wall that gets the most light, and another swath on the darkest wall. Don't neglect to prime the surface before painting, to make certain you're getting an accurate reading of the color. Wait for the paint to dry completely. Check the new color at different times of the day, both on a bright day and a dismal day. Look at the color at night with the lights on high and then on low. Talk over the choices. You'll be amazed how one color can have so many variations. If you're painting furniture, do a test where it won't show, probably the bottom of the piece. Patience rewards you with no surprises.

- **Buy expensive art and rugs on an approval-first basis.** Most dealers will allow artwork and rugs to leave their establishment, if secured by a check or credit card (requirements differ). This approval period prevents impulse-buying on your part, plus it allows for a brief road test with the piece. Intense discussion may take place in the privacy of your own home.

- **Get to know it before you buy it.** Together, look at your "on approval" purchase in its intended room. Live with it for at least a day. During this time, do not reveal your opinions or visceral responses. When it's time to talk over any potential purchase with your partner, remember that taste is a personal and subjective thing. Put-downs such as "You've got to be kidding!" or "A child could have painted that!" are not allowed. Should one person in a committed relationship declare, "It's my money, and I say 'no'!" the other partner has two choices: look for another rug, *or* look for another partner.

- **Two people working together can make a bare wall into a gallery.** A piece of artwork hung too high or too low can make me want to rehang it on the spot, which is fine if you're at home at the time. Don't forget that right under your own roof, there may be others to consider. So work with your partner to decide on an arrangement that works best for the setting, and for you. Arrange art, photos, or decorative framed pieces on the floor in the order you expect to hang them. Rearrange the position and spacing on the floor, until you're happy with it. As a rule, art is most effective when it's hung at *average* eye level, but there are many successful variations on this rule. When hanging graphic textiles, such as a patterned quilt or pictorial hooked rug, make sure the textile suits the particular space, before you go to the expense of having it mounted.

- **Make use of fabric samples.** Invest in a yard of that wild leopard-print fabric. Live with it for a full week before you decide to buy the twenty yards the job requires. One person's jungle dream is another person's nightmare. Making a throw pillow? Wrap a sample of the new fabric over an existing pillow. Prop the mock pillow in place and leave the room. Reenter and check out your "new" pillow, as though seeing it for the first time.

- **Preview wallpaper samples on the intended wall.** Ask for the largest sample the supplier is willing to provide. Tape up all the candidates, and then eliminate one at a time.

- **If a carpet sample is skimpy, let the store know you're serious about a possible purchase and ask if the store can spare a larger piece or several small samples.** Place small samples together on the floor. Run the carpet through many of the same tests you used with the paint chips. When buying a rug, ask to preview it without shoes (but with socks or stockings). This will give you an at-home sense of the rug's texture.

- **If you like to shop on-line, print out an item, preferably in color.** Many Internet sites let you enlarge individual items, from sofas to bedspreads, before you print out the page. Color printouts have taken on a unique decorating use. When you're trying to mix or match colors and patterns, use the color printouts for "samples." While it's true that color photocopies or computer printouts rarely claim a hundred percent match, they're as true as something you might clip from a catalog. Just don't be surprised when your bedspread's "sky blue" turns out to look more like periwinkle.

- **Display any artwork you're considering for purchase in a prominent spot, so that others have easy access to it.** In this way, everyone feels more involved.

- **Don't let decorating decisions bog you down.** Choosing among exquisite paint colors or shopping for the perfect chandelier is a very pleasant way to enjoy a partner's company. Working cooperatively with a child on his or her room or personal space has the potential for turning into quality time together. The experience will be far more pleasurable if you leave pressured decisions for your workplace.

- **Talk about the money, honey!** Far too many couples run into trouble when they assume that the financial aspect of home decorating will somehow take care of itself. Olivia Mellan, a psychotherapist and author of *Money Harmony,* says that most couples don't talk about finances regularly, don't share the power and decision-making, and may wind up attacking each other for differences in money styles. Avoid money conflicts by making a realistic budget

The Joy of Hanging Together

The first time Ken and I worked together to arrange a sizable grouping of our combined framed pieces (different sizes, types of frames, and media) on one long uninterrupted living room wall, I was sure any success would be a result of his strength and my experienced eye for design. In the end, it was my sense of color harmony, plus his sense of balance—combined with the patience I lack—that resulted in a perfect flow across the room.

together and setting up ground rules for spending money at the start of any project, whether it's shopping for a pillow or redoing the dining room. Address issues such as: Who will keep track of the budget? Will the financial burden be split or paid by one partner? Will you pay with a credit card or with cash? Too often, money means control, an attitude that inevitably leads to unhappiness in decorating and in life.

Domestic Kindness for Two

If your partner declares, "Well, I want brown!" and you see red, get a grip! According to psychologists, the more caring the home environment, the more likely partners are to breeze through crises, decorating and otherwise.

A lighthearted variety of thoughtful acts of domestic kindness was created by me in collaboration with my sister, Dr. Jeanne Kienzle, a psychotherapist who has counseled many couples. Use these stress busters for decorating impasses, as well as for everyday ways to put your home in a together frame of mind.

- Turn down the bedcovers on your partner's side. Fluff up the pillows, even though you'd like to toss a few out the window.
- Clean your partner's glasses. He or she will see you (and perhaps the window treatment in question) more clearly.
- Make a fire in the fireplace. The warmth of the light becomes a sign of contentment. Who knows, the two of you might even agree on the right mirror to hang above the mantel.
- A relaxed attitude is essential for home decorating decisions. "Here, put your feet up" might be the kindest words your partner has heard all day. A hassock for leg support, a small pillow for the neck, a small blanket for the lap—these are available and effortless "props" to add to your partner's comfort.
- Water the plants when it's not your job or your turn. This may be a good time to consider whether your plants really add to the room's decorative elements, or need to move to another sunny place.
- Food nourishes the body and the soul. If there's an empty space where a new dining table will go, set up a card table and plan dinner for two. Pay special attention to the selection and arrangement of food on the plates. Seasonal fruit and vegetables, such as strawberries or

artichokes, are fresh and colorful choices. Don't forget garnishes and spices with meaning: a sprig of rosemary for remembrance, garlic to ward off nasty colds (and vampires!). Often, we forget to arrange things beautifully for our own pleasure.

- If your partner longs for a hobby room or display area, track down a book about that particular interest. Instead of shrieking, "You want to hang *what kind of heads* on the walls?" ask your partner to explain why this hobby is special. Listen with an open mind and a warm heart.

- Place a newly framed photograph of your partner in plain view. Or make plans for a family rogues' gallery on one long wall, so there's room to grow.

- You like everything in its rightful place. Your partner stops and drops. Try helping out your messy partner by coming up with gadgets of order: pretty and useful boxes, special clothes hangers, plastic see-through storage bags, desk boxes, plastic holders. Place clear labels on items stored in closed crates or containers. Offer to organize his or her sock drawer. Be sure you follow your partner's logic and needs and not your own.

- Sorry you lost your temper over the size of the new TV? Make it up to your partner by programming the remote control to include his or her favorite programs. And remember that the new flat-screen TVs will come down in price eventually.

- A pretty stone from the beach or an unusual walking stick from the woods can remind partners of a happy time together. Incorporate these elements into your decor for texture and interest.

- Flower bulbs grown in glass containers become decorative reminders of renewal. Over time, watch bulbs root, leaves sprout, and buds flower.

- Decorating dilemmas making life seem too serious? Gift wrap a crystal paperweight or a snow globe for your partner. This keepsake serves as a whimsical reminder of levity.

- If your partner has a particular collection—rocks, fishing memorabilia, arrowheads, seashells—with no place to display it, search around for a see-through cabinet or suitable way to frame the collection. Present the ideas to your partner. Just the fact that you've done so much research will mean a lot.

- Has your partner left his or her usual mess? Place a little toy pig by the scene of the crime. Humor is a wonderful method to defuse a tense situation.

- Pinpoint an area of your decorating partnership where the two of you have totally different

Let two pieces, dramatically different in style, *show each other off to advantage. If you think that a simple cottage-style table desk and chair just won't work with ornate antique leaded glass, take another look.*

tastes in style, cost levels, plans, and sensibilities. Then set aside half an hour to listen to your partner's point of view with appreciation and respect. Then it's your turn to do the same.

■ Having a silly disagreement? Bring out two water pistols and go for it. Make sure that an unframed watercolor, signed by the artist and propped against the wall, is not in your line of fire.

A Useful Project: Till Design Do Us Part

Here's a lighthearted, as well as eye-opening, way to spend a rainy afternoon. If you have a clipping file, look over your choices. Get rid of anything that no longer interests you. Try to identify specific elements that work for you. Identify any design elements (colors, shapes, styles) that come up again and again. Sort your clippings into specific rooms and/or projects. Finally, choose a dozen favorites to share with your partner.

New to the art of clipping? Buy several current decorating magazines that catch your eye, or clip from any saved issues. If any male in the decorating partnership declares: "Real guys don't clip!" tell him he can *rip out* the magazine pages, if that makes him feel more comfortable about getting in closer touch with his "feminine" side. Select your favorites.

Comparing the two sets of clippings can be a real eye-opener. Often, verbal descriptions are vague and misleading. But an image allows partners to get a better sense of each other's design sensibilities. If your styles seem compatible, you're on your way. If they're not, respectfully talk about the things you like about each other's selections. Look for elements in common. Then look for the differences.

Decorating Dilemmas

A SIMPLE WAY TO HANG TOGETHER

Q: My husband and I are crazy about old quilts. Can you suggest an inexpensive and effective way to hang our favorite?

A: Hanging a quilt is rarely a solo project. But neither of you needs expert sewing skills to display a quilt securely and effectively on a wall, without damaging the textile. A wooden dowel, slipped through a cloth sleeve on the back of the quilt at the top, supports the quilt evenly. When hung over nails or wall fasteners, or on a bracket, the dowel is out of view. Here's a step-by-step guide.

1. Select a wooden dowel sufficiently strong to keep your quilt from sagging in the middle. Many hardware stores carry dowels, but lumberyards provide a wider range of sizes and lengths.

2. Many quilt experts suggest that fabric for the sleeve be cut on the bias, "bias" being the diagonal of the fabric, for more give. (An old sheet works for most quilt sleeves.) Looking for a quicker solution? Sewing supply stores carry prefolded bias tape, made wide enough for some quilt-hanging projects. No bias in sight? Use the straight of the fabric. Just make sure your sleeve, also called a "casing," is wide enough for the dowel to slip through without puckering (too tight) or bagging (too loose).

3. The sleeve should run across the back of the quilt, slightly below the top edge. You'll save time and energy if, using a warm iron, you turn under and press down a small hem on the long sides and the ends of the band before you pin or baste the sleeve in place. Start the sleeve 1 to 2 inches from the ends. The exposed portion of the dowel will hang on nails or wall fasteners. Very large and/or heavy quilts may require additional support in the center. If this is the case, leave an opening in the middle of the sleeve to expose the dowel for hanging.

4. By hand, sew the sleeve to the back of the quilt. Sorry, but machine stitching damages both old and new quilt fabric. Considering iron-on tape? Not a good idea!

5. In some cases, a dowel is needed at the bottom of the quilt for weight; hence, add a second sleeve for a second dowel.

6. Sand or cover rough ends before you slip the dowel through the quilt sleeve to protect the textile and to make the job easier.

7. Determine the right spot for the quilt. Keep in mind that textiles hung in direct light fade quickly, ruining the value of an heirloom quilt as well as preventing a new quilt from aging gracefully. Pick an interior space, or one that receives little direct or bright light. Certain window glass claims to protect against fading, but rarely does this include fragile textiles.

8. Install the most suitable wall fasteners (nail, molly bolt, bracket) for the size and weight of the quilt and the type of wall. Hang the quilt. Step back. Enjoy the view!

Some bright ideas: Shop for a curtain rod (wooden or metal) with handsome finials, such as cones, balls, or arrows, to complement your style of quilt. Or hang a happy quilt in a child's room on a wooden rod. Find a snappy color in the quilt and paint the wooden rod and finials the same color.

3
GETTING
ORGANIZED

Taking Inventory

It's time to take a good look around, as though you were seeing any and all home furnishings possessions for the very first time, including that elephantine Victorian loveseat heirloom that takes up half the room, and a large threadbare rug desperately seeking repair or replacement. If the merry mix of belongings in your home is at all similar to ours, you're eager for ways to separate the good from the bad and the ugly. Going step by step, you'll find out about commonsense ways to do a kind of spring-cleaning for home decorators. This means developing an accurate inventory of your possessions, specifically in the space you intend to redo and its related areas.

This is a perfect time to document your possessions for insurance purposes. From minor water damage to a devastating robbery, most insurance claims require accurate documentation. What better way to keep track of your belongings than with a clear photograph? A home video with commentary is often recommended for insurance purposes. However, I continue to prefer still shots for home decorating purposes. They're handier for keeping an inventory current.

Doing an Inventory

Are you moving up from milk crates to real chairs? Replacing war-torn furniture from your child-rearing days? Merging lives and furniture with a partner? Dusting off late Uncle Albert's estate? It's vital to take a careful inventory of the room—before you change, move, or buy one thing.

And before you write anything down, do a walk-through of the room, sizing up each possession—from tables to paperweights. Your sense of what fits may change as you make your decorating plan, so keep an open mind. Check out the condition of things—especially the appearance of upholstery and furniture surfaces. It looks and feels good to put things in shipshape.

As you do your walk-through, use the following questions as guidance:

- Do you want to keep it forever? (You'll find a way to make meaningful possessions work.)
- Does it have possibilities? Has it outlived its usefulness? Do you wince at the very sight of it? Do you want to donate it to charity and, if the piece has any value, gain added benefit from a tax deduction? (Be brutally honest!)

- Might it work if you had it reupholstered? Slipcovered?
- Should a particular piece be repaired? Reframed? Resilvered? Restuffed? Regilded? Repainted? Think about easy projects you can handle on your own, such as dressing up old pillows with sensational new trimming or painting worn wicker.
- Are the lines and style right for your new vision of the room?
- Are the pillows lumpier than bad oatmeal? For appearance and for comfort, upgrade to a quality synthetic fill, or inserts made of divine down or feathers and down. Pillow forms are sold through many linen catalogs. For example, Cuddledown of Maine offers premade sizes, as well as a custom service for odd-size inserts (see Resources).
- Examine the condition and effectiveness of rug pads, especially those in high-traffic areas. Replace worn or ineffective ones, because any rug on the move is an accident waiting to happen.
- Examine furniture for wobbly legs and weak seats; clocks for proper working order; lampshades for yellowing and scorch marks.
- Check the condition of all surfaces, especially those in clear view—wooden, plastic, glass, chrome, gilded, lacquer, etc.
- Remove pictures from the wall and check the condition of the frame and the back. Have acid-free mats been used with art and photography? If you're not sure, ask a reliable framer.
- Check decorative accessories for dents, nicks, rips, and fading. Look over cherished family heirlooms and antiques for needed restoration.

To Have and to Hold, or Not

With pad and pencil (no accidental ink stains!) in hand, do a written inventory. Keep things organized by dividing your list into three categories: Keeps; Rejects; Mergers and Transfers. Modify the list according to your needs and the way you like to work.

THE KEEPS

Unless you own few things to start with, or know your possessions down to the last detail, you'll want to look things over more than once. The first time 'round, be spontaneous and list things you can't live without. Then go back

For years, my grandmother's writing desk *sat in storage until I found a perfect place for it in a new home. Some possessions are worth the wait, especially those with emotional holding tags.*

Do you hang on to the good, *the bad, and the ugly, never editing even the most hopeless old loveseat? Take a look at this stylish and comfortable room, one that gives credence to the concept of "less is more."*

and double-check your choices according to your decorating dream plan for the space.

- Divide your inventory into "yes" and "maybe" possessions.
- If you intend to send certain things to storage, note those. My cherished walnut writing desk, once my grandmother's, gathered dust in a friend's attic for years, until I found the perfect setting for it in a new home.
- Create a column for any repair and/or creative redo.
- Measure every piece and record the exact measurements: H = total height (how tall the piece stands); W = total width (how long across); and D = total depth (measurement from front to back).
- Add a place for notes and reminders.
- Don't forget to consider *overall visual mass.* A heavily carved tall mahogany clock will occupy more visual volume than a simple, whitewashed tall Swedish clock, even if their measurements

Handle with Care

Delicate furniture needs placement out of the fray. I've placed a lovely but delicate wicker rocker in an upstairs hallway, where people can admire it when passing but won't be tempted to sit down. A friend stretched a fancy red tasseled tieback, meant for a floor-length curtain, across the front of a fragile antique child's rocker. It's my friend's courteous museum-inspired way to say, "Please look, but don't touch."

are fairly similar. Every piece has a real size and a *perceived size.* Other features that fool our visual perception include: bonnets, cornices, finials, "step-back" features, mirrors with prominent and elaborate frames, chunky chairs. Upholstered furniture without skirting (especially chairs and sofas with feet and legs exposed), as well as beds without dust ruffles and other skirting, appear more open and airy, as if they occupy less space than they really do.

■ Sometimes the *actual weight* must be factored in. Once a very heavy piece is set in place, it's not likely that you'll want to move it often.

■ This is the time to get acquainted with the *special needs* of certain furnishings. For example, many old or fragile textiles (quilts, rugs, needlepoint) fade in direct sunlight and so have special requirements for storage and display. Also, artwork should be treated with acid-free matting for enduring protection.

THE REJECTS

No fuss, no bother! Create a carefully considered list of things to get rid of. Whether a piece is going to a tag sale or to an auction, list it in your inventory. Create a space for:

■ Phone numbers of movers, dealers, etc.

■ Appraisal prices

■ Tax deduction slips for donated items

■ Salvation Army pickup days

■ Interested relatives

■ Garage sale plans (including prices you hope to get)

THE MERGERS AND TRANSFERS

Mergers

Taking a partner for better or worse may also mean taking his or her fake Louis IV canopied bed with matching dressers, which you'd rather not. Since both partners have vowed to live as one, you may wish to park a few possessions on this list while you decide how to redecorate.

Immediate nixes go to the Rejects list; everything else gets measured and photographed.

Transfers

This refers to possessions from a second home that might fit more effectively into your present decorating plans; it also refers to possessions in storage in need of the perfect place.

Getting Potted

Don't forget to include nature's accessories in your inventory—especially a thriving indoor tree. "Be good to them before the chaos begins," cautions Connecticut floral designer Evan Hughes. "If something needs repotting, do it well in advance to give your plant time to adjust. When making a plan that involves changing any plant's exposure, pay special attention to its special light requirements." Move houseplants to a temporary spot that's far enough away from harmful home improvement fumes and paint splashes.

Say Cheese!

Everything you plan (or hope) to use in your newly decorated space needs a mug shot and accurate measurements for reference. A point-and-shoot camera does the trick, as do the small throwaway cameras with flash, or a Polaroid. Ideally, you should:

- Start by photographing whole rooms. It's smart to have documentation of your space as it looks before redecorating. Use a simple camera, preferably one with a wide-angle setting. Stand in the middle of the floor and turn your body 360 degrees to capture the complete space.
- If at all possible, move other possessions out of the way for a clean shot.
- Photograph pieces from all the angles that are important to their placement: that is, anything you'll see or have to deal with when working with them. Special features, such as the open doors of a cupboard, a tall finial, or a TV cabinet with an open back, require special considerations up front, rather than later.
- Do a close-up shot of any special feature.
- On the photos, as well as in your inventory, note the locations of openings for outlets or wiring, especially in TVs, stereos, and computer equipment.
- Write the measurements on the back of the picture, as well as on your inventory list.
- Keep all photographs in a folder or a file, sorted by room or project. Remove shots to take along when shopping for fabric or compatible pieces.

Is It Worth More than You Think?

Antiques Roadshow Primer: The Introductory Guide to Antiques and Collectibles from the Most-Watched Series on PBS is a terrifically useful book by Carol Prisant, based on the top-rated television show. Take a look at it for the heads-up on valuable old pieces, including family belongings under wraps in closets and attics. An equally engaging paperback sequel features twentieth-century collectibles.

Label Proud

Inventory photos are more easily identified with printed labels, especially if you have an illegible handwriting like mine. I'm an avid fan of the electronic label-maker. The bold black letters on white label tape reveal necessary documentation at a glance (they tell me what's *inside* file boxes). Plus, this system makes me *feel* more organized.

Making Space to Work

Not everyone has an attic, basement, or storage area. Even the roomy storage barn at our farm is limited to solid surfaces, as the upholstered items are discovered quickly by the mice. If you're redoing a large space and have run out of corners, closets, and willing friends, consider renting a temporary ministorage unit. This can run up your budget; however, many self-storage units have reasonable fees, so shop around. Be sure to photograph and document *everything* that goes into storage. If anything is stolen or damaged, you'll have a record for insurance claim purposes.

A Useful Project: Is It Gem or Rubbish?

Even if you're not involved at present in a home decorating project, begin an inventory for insurance purposes. In this way, a kind of rainy-day inventory is ready when you are. Begin by tackling nesting spaces in need of renewal. Go on to other rooms of the house. You'll accomplish this important project list by list, and photo by photo.

Decorating Dilemmas

ORGANIZATIONALLY CHALLENGED

Q: I'm too young to be senile, but I seem to have the worst memory when my projects aren't in front of my nose. As soon as I put a fabric sample in a drawer, it's history. I'd like to take on several rooms in our new house, but I need a decorating file that will work. I've got great ideas, once I can find them.

A: Your problem is one that many of us face: the need to *see* things (clues and reminders), as well as a need to get at them easily. Custom-make a system that lets things find you.

For example, set aside a space in a closet you don't ignore (your clothes closet or a frequently used hall closet are likely candidates). Hang "file cabinets" in the form of durable canvas sweater racks, handy clothing "pockets," crystal-clear plastic storage boxes, and open baskets. Home stores and catalogs sell many items that can double for project storage. A series of clear plastic windows on a hanging bag intended for jewelry will keep track of small, easily misplaced samples, such as decorative trimming, ribbon, buttons, and tassels.

A large bulletin board is a good investment as a place to tack up a super-size calendar and project schedule. There's a kind of reminder board that comes outfitted with crisscrossed bands of elastic—handy for tucking in notes, photos, and small clippings.

When it comes to storing piles of samples (fabrics, wallcoverings, rugs) in plain view, organize them in jumbo food storage bags, the clear plastic ones with sturdy plastic zippers. Use empty shoeboxes for samples, too. Line them up on an open shelf, topless and labeled boldly.

If you want to get fancy, there are plenty of pretty cardboard storage boxes at affordable prices. I got mine at Target. Keeping track of things is just a matter of finding your organizing groove.

4 CHECKING OUT
THE BONES

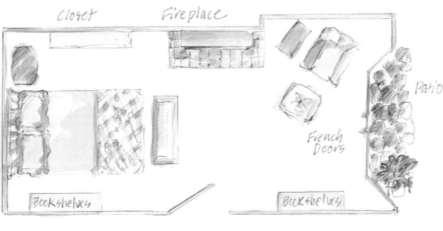

Closet Fireplace

Patio

French
Doors

Bookshelves

Bookshelves

Bones

You may have heard someone say that a house, or a room, has "good bones." This term is not used exclusively to describe grand old houses or expensively renovated spaces. The "bones" are the basic structural features (also called "architectural features") of a particular house or building. Bones might include an especially large and attractive window, a door with the old carving still intact, mellow pine floors, grooved wood paneling, or a fireplace. Good bones make up the character of the space.

The various features may be broken down into logical categories, such as:

- Room size and shape
- Windows and doors
- Walls and ceilings
- Floors
- Special architectural features (meaning unusual structural elements, such as a stone fireplace, a pair of columns, or a handcrafted stairway banister)

If you're thinking "My room needs a total face-lift!" take heart. This chapter offers ways to find the strengths and weaknesses of any room by making it into a kind of blank working canvas. Often, it's possible to use visual tricks to diminish the impact of an unsightly feature, without making major changes. One Greenwich Village apartment-dweller came up with a layered look for a living room window to camouflage a monstrous metal security gate that pulls across the entire window to block access from a fire escape. She pulled floor-to-ceiling curtains back into graceful folds, then hung a delicate matchstick shade in front of the security gate. The shade covers the eyesore, yet it allows light to filter through. Two other windows in the room have matching window treatments.

Finding the Words

What impresses you about the overall space? What depresses you? Verbalize your feelings with a partner or a friend, as though you're giving them a tour of the space. Then find one word or a brief phrase to describe your total sense of the bones. Kick off your thinking with this list of possible descriptions:

- ❏ Dismal?
- ❏ Filled with characteristic details?
- ❏ Cut up?
- ❏ Cavernous?

❑ Plain and boxy?　　　　　　　　　❑ Dramatic?

❑ Open, with clean lines?　　　　　　❑ Add your own word: _____

Before you start any decorating project, find one word that describes the way the present room looks.

❑ Cluttered?　　　　　　　　　　　❑ Drab?

❑ Bare?　　　　　　　　　　　　　❑ Pleasant?

❑ Homey?　　　　　　　　　　　　❑ Stiff?

❑ Dated?　　　　　　　　　　　　❑ Add your own word: _____

This quick exercise is intended to help you see the structural features more clearly, as well as to review the effect of how any space has been changed or altered permanently.

Identifying Focal Points

When you walk into the empty room, what do you see first? What is a dominant structural element? This is your structural focal point (or architectural focal point). The wall opposite the entry is the focal wall. If your view is of a lovely brick fireplace, or a pair of double doors that open onto a well-tended garden, your focal point is a favorable one. If you're confronted with a view of your neighbor's run-down garage, you may need to shift the focus, improve it, or camouflage it. A room's structural focal point may include:

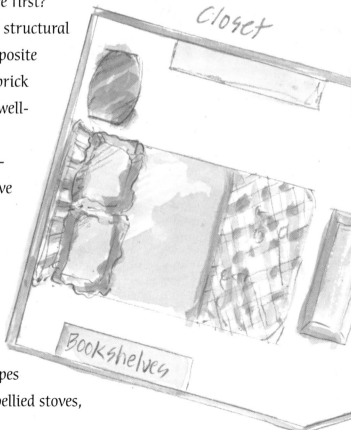

■ A fireplace

■ Prominent windows, such as a bay window

■ Prominent doors and doorways, such as French doors

■ Structural elements, such as columns and fixed pipes

■ Heating and cooling units, such as radiators, potbellied stoves, and air conditioners

■ Beams and rafters

The fireplace in this cozy room *is the first thing visitors see when they enter. The homeowner has taken advantage of what might have been a gaping, dark focal point by adding unusual decorative elements in and around it.*

- Unusual features, such as a conversation pit
- Structural nooks and alcoves
- Permanent built-in furniture, such as bookcases and storage units
- A fixed mirrored surface
- Dropped ceilings and other unusual ceiling features
- Recessed lighting and other built-in lighting features, including less obvious sources, such as overhead lighting that may be part of a ceiling fan

By taking note of your room's prominent structural elements, you'll be in a better position to recognize a suitable problem-solving idea when it comes your way.

Tips of the Trade

If cozy is what you're after in a small room, paint the walls a rich, dark color—a forest green, mysterious mauve, warm melon. Add a chunky love seat or a matching pair of club chairs. Full doesn't always mean "crowded." Combining darker colors and large-scale furniture can make a room feel comfortable as well as dignified.

Closet Play

In search of a guest bathroom during a party, I opened the wrong door. There in front of me was a family of bears. Alas, it was simply the doors of a wide closet on the other side of the room, transformed by a whimsical trompe l'oeil scene of three bears sleeping *inside* the closet. What might have been a dead-end focal point in a child's bedroom had become magical. A nearby door led to the bathroom, a room rather ordinary by comparison.

Size Matters!

Yes, the size of a room, as well as its shape, matters very much. On paper, a seemingly claustrophobic living space may just be overcrowded with furniture and what all of us refer to as "stuff." And if you have to deal with an unsightly exposed radiator, it may well seem far larger than it is after it's measured. Every element needs closer inspection.

Evaluating Size and Shape

Don't hunt for the measuring tape just yet. Begin by using your mind's eye to scope out your space for its size. Although this is better done on site, it's a thinking part of your decorating plan. In fact, I've done some of my best room plans on planes and trains. Make informal notes for yourself, using the following points for guidance:

Does the room serve as an appropriate and useful space for its intended purpose? Most of us don't think of our homes as museums, yet we overlook opportunities to take advantage of wasted or little-used space. For example, an infrequently used dining room might be put to better use, especially for a growing family, as a casual living area—for meals, to watch TV, or to enjoy hobbies. If you think a designated space for special dining will be missed, consider a drop-leaf table for another area—a spacious hallway or an open part of the living room. The table can be opened and used where it is, or moved into another space. The key is flexibility.

Does a certain room feel too large? Wonder how you'll ever fill it, or warm it up? Here are possible solutions to consider:

A small dining room *has been opened up with beautiful and simple old furniture; its polished patina reflects the light from attractively unadorned windows. A handcrafted chandelier made of sheet metal becomes a dramatic focal point.*

- Plan for at least one commanding piece: a tall chest of drawers, floor-to-ceiling bookshelves, or a grandfather clock.

- Use the same prominent window treatment for all windows in the same space to help pull the area together.

- Paint the walls a deep, rich color for a more homey feeling.

- Break up your big space with a room divider—a fabulous painted screen, a gigantic English pine plate rack, a long bench.

- Create several seating areas, and make sure there's one for more intimate conversation.

- Hang terrific poster art or a large painting on a prominent wall, preferably the wall you see when you enter the room. Illuminate the artwork with a unique picture light. This light attaches to the top of the frame or to the wall. The electrical cord hangs straight to the floor, unless a high wall socket has been installed for it. Visually, artwork pulls a wall more into the space, while the soft picture light above it further cozies up the room.

- Paint one wall a darker, or different, color. This adds interest and warmth.

Does the room feel uncomfortably small?

- Open it up with a pale tone-on-tone color scheme throughout.
- Hang framed artwork on the longest wall. Then set decorative objects—baskets, ceramic bowls, small sculptures—on a low bench or shelf running the length of the same wall. This decorates any space without adding more than eight to twelve inches to it.
- Paint the ceiling white, or a lighter shade of white than the walls.
- Select window treatments that allow the maximum amount of natural light—simple shades, café curtains, traditional sheers, top treatments only, or no treatment at all. Light makes spaces seem larger.
- Hang mirrors on a wall. If there's a pleasant outside view, or an especially pleasing feature in the same area, reflect it. Mirroring expands any space.

Is the room cut up into odd shapes by a dropped ceiling, different levels, eaves, dormers, low walls (also called "knee walls"), or a sleeping loft? Unify the different small spaces by using:

- Simple, streamlined wall-to-wall carpeting.
- A rug theme, created by using decorative handcrafted or antique rugs, with compatible designs and colors.
- A continuous or repeated architectural feature (chair rail, wainscoting, paneling).
- A wallpaper border can be used to connect spaces. If your room is cut up into many nooks and crannies, use the border just below where the ceiling meets the walls. Remember that any high border treatment will make the ceiling feel lower, so evaluate the height of the room before you attempt to connect the areas. Otherwise, you run the risk of feeling like Chicken Little when she cried, "The sky is falling, the sky is falling!" Borders applied at chair-rail level connect spaces as well, with or without the actual wooden trim in place.
- Built-in shelving can be designed to run around corners without a break, providing a substantial library look.

What is the traffic pattern, or flow, of your room furnished? Unfurnished? Depending on the position of the door (or doors) of a room, the shape of the space, and the location of prominent features, every room has an evident traffic pattern—that is, the way people move through it. Will you need to modify this traffic pattern? The placement of furniture and the use of the space can make a difference between having privacy to carry on a conversation and dealing with an annoying parade. A few solutions:

■ Keep furniture clear of an active door.

■ Plan to place a TV away from high-traffic areas, especially kid-gathering spots.

■ Make sure there's a simple pathway to desks, beds, favorite chairs. Climbing over ottomans and slapping at tall potted plants are not a part of the plan.

Examining a Room's Elements

Now that you've looked critically at the room as a whole, it's time to look at the individual elements of the same space. The idea is to identify anything that you may wish to change, and then decide on the right plan to achieve the change. Careful notes (for your eyes only!) provide a useful record. The type of elements you'll be looking at include some of the following:

■ The style of window treatments

■ The color of your room

■ Where you will place delicate vintage textiles

■ Where and where not to place furniture

■ The need for particular lighting and lamps

WINDOWS AND DOORWAYS

What is the main function of individual windows?

■ Light?

■ Ventilation?

■ Leading to a fire escape?

■ A fabulous view?

Does the placement of windows seem balanced? Is it pleasing to your sense of the total room?

Are the windows attractive? Attractive enough to be left bare? Will you need to hide unattractive window features?

Are windows too high or too low for the space? For your decoration plans?

Do you have the privacy you need, or will you have to create it? Obviously, this is most important in a bedroom and a bathroom.

What is your initial vision for a window treatment?

- Curtains?
- Shades?
- Top treatment only (such as a cornice or a simple swag)?
- A simple privacy shade?
- Nothing at all?

Notice the room's exposure. Which direction does the light come from—north, south, east, or west?

Does the room have a single exposure or multiple exposures? What is the direction of each exposure? How will this affect your use of space?

Is the natural light blocked by trees part of the year or year round? Does the window look out at another house, a tall building, or a brick wall? (Prospective home buyers should open every curtain and shade in prospective houses for a true picture of the natural light.)

Does your room have broad mood swings? Jot down the quality of the light. Return to the room at different times of the day. Check it on drab days and on sunny days.

What is the main function of individual doorways?

- Active passageway?
- Entrance to a dark and narrow hallway?
- More decorative than functional?

Do the windows and doorways, taken together, make the room seem:

- Light and airy?
- Cozy and warm?
- Cheerless?

Is a doorway too wide and awkward? You could drape it with curtains for an exotic, romantic, or Victorian look. If the light is right, bank wide doorways with potted palms to create the illusion of a garden gate. Build narrow shelving for books and/or small objects to run the height of the doorway—on one side only or on both sides, depending on clearance considerations. Extend the shelving across the top of the door frame.

Are your doors too plain? Apply a thin molding strip several inches in from the edges, creating a center panel design. Paint everything the same color; paint the molding a different, brighter color for a pop; or paint the door in contrasting faux finishes. Enhance painted doors with many of the same techniques used on walls and ceilings.

SCALING THE WALLS

What shape are your walls in? Will a little spackle do it? If you've budgeted for a more structural makeover, special linen wall covering can be applied to the walls after spackling and before final painting. This durable material promises to cover cracks and crevices indefinitely, taking years off the age of the wall. A professional painter should do this, though.

Sometimes flaws can add to various decorative faux finishes on walls. Check out ragging, sponging, and color-washing in the many good books devoted to the subject. Consult at least one detailed source before tackling the job on your own. There are a number of useful specialty books, including *New Paint Magic* by Jocasta Innes.

If the fall of Rome is your style, employ a skilled artist to paint frescoes to enhance the effect; otherwise, it might look more like a visual aid from your child's history assignment.

If you're not happy with your wood paneling, it can be painted over—with a color or with white. Just remember: There are *many* shades of white.

Does a partially exposed brick wall tempt you to find out what's underneath the entire wall? It may pay to uncover a wall's natural beauty. You can buy new bricks to cover plain walls. Most are far thinner than regular bricks, and some are made of synthetic material. All bricking involves a good deal of work and time on the handy person's part.

A variety of wall coverings is available—from fabric to charming patterned and textured wallpaper—to cover up flaws, while creating a particular mood.

Is there a long wall for your sofa? If not, don't worry. Sometimes, sofas can look more interesting when they're placed:

- Away from the wall
- On the diagonal
- In front of a window
- In the center of the room
- Opposite the fireplace, or flanking a fireplace in a love seat arrangement

Will large artwork or wall hangings have a suitable home on the existing wall space? If your wall space is limited and your ceiling is low, you could:

- Place more prominent works of art on the floor, leaning *against* a wall. This is an effective, if somewhat trendy, notion that works best with bold images. A heavy piece might be bolted to the wall, especially in a home where small children might get hurt.
- Display pictures on small desk easels placed on a mantel.
- Position the right balance of artwork on a bookshelf to add interest, enhance colorful book jackets and decoratively imprinted book spines, and break up a long row of rather ordinary-looking books. On a shelf for displaying collectible treasures, a picture becomes the focal point that ties the arrangement together.
- Be on the lookout for an artist's easel (many old easels are carved and made of beautiful wood), preferably a large one that stands firmly. When the easel is displayed in an effective spot, with the artwork in place, people are inclined to walk right up to it for a closer look. Modern artwork on an elaborately adorned Victorian easel often results in a striking contrast of styles.

DON'T FORGET TO LOOK UP

Is the ceiling too high?

- Use a colorful or detailed border to lower the ceiling. Often, borders painted to resemble decorative molding fool the eye into thinking the molding is the real thing.
- Paint the ceiling a dark color or a tint of the wall color to bring it down a notch visually.
- Get rid of the sharp line where the wall paint color and the lighter ceiling meet by extending your wall color beyond the ceiling line approximately four inches to create a narrow border. The result is a subtle but effective way to lower the sense of a too-high ceiling.
- Plaster beams can be painted with a faux decorative painting technique to resemble wooden beams.

Is the ceiling too low?

- Makeup artists advise women to put blush high on their cheekbones, as well as ever so lightly on their foreheads, for an uplifting effect. If you're using a color wash on your walls, it's easy to use the same principle to "lift" the ceiling. The change must be subtle, made only as higher sections of wall are being worked on. To avoid a visible line, darken the paint just a hint, washing it softly and letting your eye guide you. A variety of color-wash techniques, as well as sponging, allows the painter to take advantage of the lift. Don't try this on walls painted a solid color.

A Jeffersonian Thought

Whenever I pass through Virginia's Charlottesville–Albemarle Airport, I pause as soon as I enter the lobby rotunda and look up. Elegantly scrolled there are the eloquent and enduring words of Thomas Jefferson. I read slowly, pausing at,

"Never can we overestimate the great value of our hard-won freedom. I am happy nowhere else, and in no other society, and all my wishes end, where I hope my days will end, at Monticello. Too many scenes of happiness mingle themselves with all the recollections of my native woods and fields to suffer them to be supplanted in my affection by any other."

Calligraphy and thoughtful words need not be limited to notable statesmen and public places. A homespun Jeffersonian takeoff is to stencil or scroll inspirational words, ideas, or sayings in a special space, border-style. Make sure you outline in pencil, have a steady hand, and possess the perseverance of Leonardo da Vinci, especially if the goal is to lower the entire ceiling visually. For a less physically stressful option, place your words on a simple wallpaper border, perhaps a marbleized design, and then apply the border.

- Hang a curtain on a rod *above* the top of a window or glass doors. The right height for the rod is what looks right to you.
- Display an eye-catching collection—decorative plates, flat baskets, African masks—in a line high on a prominent wall to fool the eye.
- To avoid sharp contrasts between ceiling and walls, hang a neutral wallpaper border around the edge of the ceiling where it meets the wall.

If you're stuck with an unattractive electrical cover in the center of the ceiling where a light used to be:

- Create your own design for a ceiling medallion, or buy a ready-made stencil. Intricate geometric designs and stars are especially popular. They're available at craft, housewares, and home decorating stores.
- Investigate the work of metal artisans at shows and in crafts magazines for a one-of-a-kind chandelier. (The American Crafts Council has a Web site at www.craftcouncil.org, where

you'll find a listing of their first-rate retail shows. In addition, you'll find the work of many talented artisans who create furniture and accessories in every possible area of home design.)

■ Change your old ceiling fixture (or that dull pendant light) by refinishing it to mimic gilding or verdigris. Prepackaged paint kits are available at hardware and paint stores.

If you decide to change the look of the entire ceiling, you can:

■ Combine wallpaper and borders for a canopy effect.

■ Create a dramatic tentlike effect with fabric. (Not recommended for the novice.)

■ Find heavy paper sheets that have been hot-pressed (or embossed) with designs resembling old tin ceilings, as well as decorative molding. Much like wallpaper, the sheets are pasted in place before painting.

■ Create a loose stucco effect with a ready-made stucco mix.

■ Look into easy-to-apply cardboard and plastic molding strips, pressed into a variety of convincing relief designs. Placed just below the ceiling and painted as trim (or the same color as the ceiling), these impostors look like the real thing.

LITTLE THINGS COUNT

When I painted the very plain wooden knobs of an unremarkable pine dresser with a high-gloss black, the look of the piece smartened up beyond anything I'd imagined. Often, changing a seemingly insignificant detail makes all the difference.

■ Upgrade any ill-suited or shoddy-looking hardware. Brass and pewter knobs and pulls add distinction to traditional pieces. Or perhaps you're inclined to seek out hardware of a more whimsical bent: spoon-shaped drawer pulls, flower-inspired hooks, acornlike knobs for cabinet doors.

■ Cover unsightly switch plates and outlet covers with the same wallpaper used on the walls. Or replace them with their decorative metal counterparts; buy plain white, or paint the offenders so that they blend in with the wall color. Caution: Never paint over plug openings. The painter runs a risk of sealing electrical plugs, plus it's never safe to work around live wires.

■ Unless you're confident and skilled enough to handle the waxing and polishing of dull hardwood floors on your own, hire a professional to bring out a floor's original luster. Soiled carpets, rugs, and upholstered items benefit from a professional cleaning as well.

Remember This

Dark and/or flat finishes, as well as textured surfaces, absorb light. Light and/or glossy finishes, as well as smooth surfaces, reflect light.

A Useful Project: Bones to Pick

Make a list of the "good bones" and the "bad (or simply mediocre) bones" of one room of your home. Leave space to jot down possible ideas and solutions to your problem area.

Decorating Dilemmas

No Bones

Q: I live in a spacious L-shaped studio apartment, a rental, that's devoid of basic charm. Without spending a lot of money on permanent improvements, how can I create a bedroom area without building a wall?

A: Assuming you own a regular bed, as opposed to a sleeper sofa or studio bed, start by finding a space for your "bedroom," hopefully out of view of the entrance. Tall privacy screens range from light and functional (cloth, straw, rice paper) to high works of art (antique Chinese lacquer, painted canvas, fancy decoupage, fabric-paneled bamboo). A chest-high dresser or bookcase might be effective in separating a sleeping area, without cutting off the flow of heat and air. Another idea is to hang a sheer curtain (or length of fabric, outfitted with rings for hanging) from a traverse rod that has been installed in the ceiling. This means that your total space can be opened up with the pull of a cord. The sheer fabric keeps you from feeling closed in.

Lengths of funky doorway beads work for some. Then there's mosquito netting for the *Out of Africa* look.

Industrial Chic

Q: My prewar apartment is filled with old steam pipes no longer in active service, water pipes that rise from floor to ceiling in odd places, and very active heating pipes. Are there ways to decorate pipes, or at least minimize their intrusion?

A: If a pipe provides heat, consider wrapping it with thin and sleek aluminum sheeting or with another suitable and attractive insulation material. Nonoperational pipes, often encrusted with a rich history of white paint, might be painted a more pleasing color, even wrapped in brown corrugated paper. A particular Asian-style restaurant I like has made their industrial floor-to-ceiling pipes into exotic bamboo poles by wrapping them with inexpensive window blinds, cut to fit, and then lashed in place with a rough brown rope. Wallpapering pipes and poles is a possibility, but a climbing ivy design may come off as just plain corny. Creating a classic striped barber's pole, using red and white tape, could be fun in a child's room or play space.

5

PROFESSIONAL
STYLE-SAVERS

For time-deprived individuals of all ages, consulting an outside expert, someone who shares your taste and vision, may be an option. The best time to think about using a professional is at the very beginning of a decorating project. The specialties and qualifications of design professionals vary, as do their titles. You're probably familiar with the terms "interior decorator" and "interior designer." Expect to come across a wide range of titles and talents, including design consultant, design specialist, color consultant, and decorative stylist.

Maximizing the potential of your space may be done more effectively in concert with a responsible professional. A trained interior designer is especially helpful on more complex design matters. He or she will be able to come up with quick solutions to get you out of hot water, assume a supporting role in your decorating life, direct trades people, and open doors to the many "trade-only" showrooms for home decorating purchases.

The Redecorators Come to Call

Today, it's possible to call in a  consultant for specific design dilemmas, for fresh ideas for change, or to carry through the entire project. Decorating consultants of this nature are referred to as "restylers" and "redecorators," or just "home stylists." An article in the *New York Times* called them "makeover medics."

Most redecorators offer flat-fee, one-day decorating services—more or less, according to your wishes and needs. The high-energy talent will (among a long list of services) suggest paint colors, rearrange furniture, hang or rehang your pictures, and display your decorative accessories to advantage. They will not walk your dog, but one redecorator helped clients design a clever setting for their dog's bed.

After you've hired a redecorator, the clock will be ticking when he or she is on the job. There's no time-out period for indecision. Maximize the time spent together by becoming a quick study.

A Designer Checklist

If you find yourself seeking out the right interior designer or design consultant, keep certain things in mind:

Designing Friends

Sometimes, the "expert" is a talented friend who can bring a breath of fresh air to your all-too-familiar room. My friend Charlotte claims that her natural eye for arranging furniture rarely works in her own home, yet it's worked miracles in mine. When she's stuck with her own decorating schemes, she calls on me. We go on shopping excursions to discount fabric stores and out-of-the-way antique shops, where we hunt for the overlooked gems at bargain prices. It's especially fun when you "connect" with a designing sidekick.

- Make your plans, tastes, and needs clear from the start.

- Keep your radar humming to evaluate whether you and the expert are on the same wavelength. If a certain designer is best known for tone-on-tone schemes and you can't live without vibrant colors, think again. The right person is someone who understands your needs and appreciates your tastes and choices, even if he or she might not do things in exactly the same way.

- Ask to see photos of recent projects. The images will give you a good sense of an interior designer's particular style. Although many interior designers say that their style on a decorating project reflects the preferences of the client, it's natural for anyone to feel inclined toward certain looks, colors, and pieces.

- Don't be intimidated by a designer who informs you haughtily that a trendy new table surface is the *only* one worth considering. Or someone whose sole message is that keeping up with the neighbors will require a substantial budget. You may think to yourself, "Well, what do I know?" The answer is: *more than you think you know!*

- If it's apparent that the designer/client combo is not in sync, make it a short conversation and move on. An initial brief consultation is essential before you sign up for anything. Most often, this consultation is free of charge, but do ask.

- Find out if friends whose homes you admire can recommend someone for your job. Your friends will appreciate the compliment.

Teaming up with the right design professional can be energizing as well as useful. Be happy with your choice.

The Skinny on Fees

The customary fee of a typical interior designer varies in different parts of the country, but fee structure tends to fall into three categories. However, keep in mind that there is no hard-and-fast rule. Be sure to ask money questions well in advance—before you start a project or shop up a storm with your new design consultant. The three main fee structures:

- A fee basis (per hour/day/job)
- A percentage of the wholesale cost of items purchased added on as the interior designer's fee (for instance, if $6,000 were spent on materials, you would expect to pay between $600 and $1,800 on top of that to the designer)
- A combination of the above

It's important to get a contract. If there's an up-front fee or a retainer, find out exactly how much and when it gets applied. Don't be surprised to find your deposit held until the final bill is paid. As with any contract, read it before you sign. It may not be as momentous as your new mortgage agreement, but it's a legally binding document.

Tune in to the A.S.I.D.

Most legitimate interior designers have undergone extensive training and are qualified to communicate on a technical level with everyone from the paint salesperson to the architect. Often, the letters "A.S.I.D." follow a designer's name on printed business stationery and business cards. This indicates that the person belongs to the American Society of Interior Designers and has met this professional organization's requirements. If networking among friends doesn't provide the right names, contact the A.S.I.D. (800-610-2743) to obtain the names of bona fide interior designers in your area. Also, go to the Web site www.interiors.org. And again:

- Be sure to ask questions about the person's training, background, and experience, especially if you're depending on him or her to see you through a whole-house treatment.
- Most established interior designers keep a portfolio that contains photographs of their jobs. Ask to look through it. Make sure you like the design styles you see there. Many design professionals are eclectic; however, you should be able to spot a certain theme or taste factor common to the different jobs.

■ Ask for references. Be sure to follow up and phone more than one person.

What if a design professional doesn't tote official certification? Many self-taught interior designers are extremely talented and capable. No need to rule out someone you like just because that person doesn't have a framed diploma hanging on the wall. However, do ask the same questions. In addition, find out if the person has access to trade showrooms and to the trades-people you'll need. In the end, you may choose to work with a talented acquaintance, perhaps someone who runs a design business during the children's school hours. Just be sure you like their work.

Who Is What?

Decorator or interior designer? Designer or design consultant? Look on a professional's business card for a title. Most of the qualified experts don't appreciate the term "decorator." One indignant acquaintance fumed, "It makes us sound like a bunch of frivolous pillow fluffers!"

Home Decorating vs. Home Improvement

For the purposes of this book, we defined "home decorating" as *transforming* a room in smart and creative ways. If you can move it or do it yourself, it's probably decorating. Jobs requiring serious renovation or construction work, such as moving a wall, lowering a ceiling, or installing new windows, fall under "home improvement." Many interior designers have the training to handle both aspects of the job.

Knowing the Ropes of Trade-Only Shopping

In most major cities, there's a design center or cluster of design wholesalers. This private shopping mall of sorts is where a range of furnishings and home accessories, from decorative tassels to marble fireplace surrounds, are displayed in spacious, and often beautifully appointed, showrooms.

Certain showrooms are very strict and exclusive. Others are kinder to walk-ins. With or without an escort, you may discover another wonderful, if more expensive, shopping source. If you do, it's a good idea to know the trade rules ahead of time.

- Don't pretend to be an interior designer shopping for a client. Impostors might as well be wearing lampshades on their heads. Be honest about the circumstances of your visit. The worst that can happen? You'll be invited to return with a professional escort, a card-carrying interior designer, who will have wholesale accounts with many of the manufacturers.
- Some showrooms have a more relaxed policy. If you don't have a child in a stroller, or a container of coffee in your hand, they may let you stroll through the showroom to window-shop. As a rule, even the more relaxed showrooms won't allow you to buy at wholesale prices.
- You'll find small printed memo pads and pencils placed conveniently at the front. These are intended to be used to jot down the style number, price (sometimes only the wholesale price is given; the retail price will be higher), and other relevant information given on the floor samples.
- In most fabric and wall-covering showrooms, you're allowed to take out something called a "memo"—a large marked sample—provided that an interior designer has phoned ahead or given you his or her business card and/or account number to show. This is similar to borrowing a library book. Memos must be returned, or the designer may be charged for them.
- Many showrooms allow nontrade shoppers to request a cutting—a small sample of fabric or wall covering. As a rule, cuttings need not be returned.
- The occasional showroom may offer to open a temporary account for you. If you're crazy about a particular showroom's lines, it pays to ask, especially if you're doing a whole-house project. If you're allowed to make a purchase on your own, it will probably be on a pro forma basis (ahead of time for each order) or COD.

What's in Their Bag?

Most successful interior designers keep careful track of decorating projects at every stage. They keep essential information such as plans, measurements, and estimates handy and up-to-date. As anyone who's redone a room knows, it's a detail-oriented business, requiring the talent of a juggler and the stamina of a long-distance runner. So take a lesson from the experts by setting up a system that works for you. Unfortunately, a project can get out of hand and out of budget faster than you can say "I'll take two."

A Traveling File and Organized Routine

It's advisable to keep important papers, as well as the smaller work-in-progress samples, in a three-ring notebook, so that decorating projects don't turn into a three-ring circus. Forget about most of the prepackaged decorating notebooks that look pretty. They make nice gifts, but they probably don't handle organization the way you do. Tailor a system that works.

Some people like to keep everything in computer files and then print out a hard copy for a "traveling file" for meetings and shopping. Others find it helpful to tack visual charts and reminders on a bulletin board. An up-to-date "to do" list keeps things moving. I keep an "action" list on my computer, and I take great joy in hitting the delete key. Here are more suggestions for keeping track of things:

- Use a loose-leaf binder that fits into your tote. Call it your "traveling file." When you need to travel even lighter, remove only the pages you'll need. Buy the handy plastic ringed pockets to hold samples, as well as heavy cardboard dividers to separate categories (kept current), such as:

  Budget

  Work orders/contracts/confirmations

  Schedule

  Floor plan

  Room measurements

  Furniture measurements

  Photos

  Sources

  Phone/fax/e-mail (important home decorating contacts only)

  Catalogs/Web sites of interest

  Relevant clippings

- Transfer things you're not using right now from your traveling file into your permanent files, kept at home. I prefer cardboard file boxes or wicker baskets especially made for hanging files. They're light, portable, and you can get them from Hold Everything and other container stores.

- Keep extra samples in a pretty box or a sturdy basket. I've pressed a charming picnic basket into service, as well as wallpaper-covered hatboxes. I treat attractive storage containers like decorative objects for the office.

■ Stack your favorite magazines on a shelf for easy reference, spines showing. If you're a type-A personality, you'll probably arrange them by title and date.

Remember that your files will expand and change, according to your decorating load and the stage of the project.

Eye-Opening Sample Boards

The sample board—it's one of the best tricks of the decorator's trade. A large sheet of plain white poster board serves as a neutral background on which to display the different colors, textures, and patterns under consideration for a particular room. They are essential tools for checking the harmony (or possible design contradictions) of any room.

Some professional designers take a rather casual approach with established clients and toss memos, cuttings, and paint chips onto the client's carpet or table. But others continue to rely on sample boards as they develop a scheme for presentation. It's easy to create your own sample boards.

■ Use double-sided tape for easy changes.

■ Keep all fabric and wallpaper samples under consideration; label them carefully with store, width, price, and repeat of pattern. Otherwise, you may find that your first choice of linen for the club chair is also the mystery fabric, found in a pile on your desk.

■ Size every sample (paint chips, fabric samples, floor coverings) in proportion to the space it will occupy in your room. That is, a bold yellow fabric sample for the sofa should be proportionately larger than the blue fabric for the accent pillow; an architectural border will show you more if it's run across the top of the board.

■ Let logic dictate. For example, if you're thinking of painting a large room a dramatic shade of blue, paint the entire sample board the room color. In this way, you're in a better position to see how other colors and textures play against the dominant background. A tiny paint chip would be misleading.

■ Get inventive! Include bits of trimming, flowerpot shards to represent terra-cotta flooring, a photo of anything large and prominent (such as a strongly patterned rug).

■ Tape the ends of trimming samples so they don't unravel.

■ Clip color pictures from magazines to use as samples.

■ If you're considering a rug or large textile, ask if a photo or picture is available.

- Take a close snapshot of anything large with a pattern or dominant color—floor tiles, painted furniture, wall hangings, and bold artwork. Make a good color photocopy of a favorite fabric sample that's on loan from a decorator showroom. Even if the colors aren't reproduced exactly, a close match will serve the purpose.
- Work with as few or as many samples as catch your imagination. Move them around in different combinations, until you find one that works for you. Then secure the samples in place, using double-sided tape. Modify your board as new and improved ideas develop.

WHAT'S THE BIG IDEA?

Sample boards may be used for a variety of design comparisons:

- The compatibility of pattern and color in one room only.
- The flow of the different paint colors from room to room.
- The harmony and balance of all colors, patterns, and textures in a particular space.

A Useful Project: Cut and Paste

Create a sample board for one room. If you're not currently planning to decorate, plan the room of your dreams on paper.

Decorating Dilemmas

ON THE CHEAP

Q: I have an empty dining room, love to cook for friends, but have no money for an interior designer. I'm into simple lines and lively colors, and I'm fairly handy. I could use an idea or two.

A: Before you begin a major do-it-yourself project, it might pay to run a few ideas past a redecorator for troubleshooting. Since you seem to have a sense of what you're looking for, the hourly rate of a redecorator may be money well spent. Being able to brainstorm with an "expert" at the start, such as color combinations, furniture styles, and layout, can save you from a project overrun, meaning going over your intended budget. And a redecorator will respect your desire to handle the actual project alone.

In the meantime, have you considered buying unpainted or stripped chairs, matched or mixed-and-matched, and painting each chair a different color? Make sure the design lines of the chairs are strong and the construction is solid. Make your mix as bright as gumballs (sounds like you!) or as subtle as nature's winter beauty (pine green, sky gray, silhouetted black, berry ocher). And make sure you're happy with the combination of colors. Since gloss paint can be difficult to apply smoothly unless it's sprayed on, I opt for a flat paint finish as it's so much easier to apply a smooth coat. Then I use a glossy nonyellowing urethane finish over the color for protection and sheen.

Simple painted chairs are especially handsome when paired with a starkly modern table. Stainless steel, tubular chrome, glass, and good-looking synthetic materials, used for tabletops, are common elements found in today's office furniture. If you're curious, go to the furniture section of a Viking Office Products or Staples catalog (see Resources). A conference table with handsome lines and plenty of room for seating may work for you, and at a price more affordable than traditional furniture.

If you have little space and lots of friends, check out modern stacking chairs for office environments. Some chairs are so well designed that you may decide to hang them high on wall pegs, Shaker-style.

6

Measuring Up
with a Floor Plan

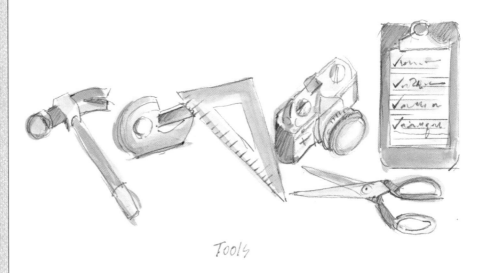

TOOLS

Laying Out the Room

An accurate basic floor plan will tell you if a wall is long enough for that king-size bed (with *both* night tables) and if you've allowed for comfortable space around furniture. Even if pieces fit into a particular space, a layout helps you determine if the tall clock *and* that substantial armoire will unbalance the room if placed on the same wall. If you change from one sofa to two facing love seats, laying out the new arrangement on the floor plan is the safest way to get a heads-up.

Does a precise floor plan sound like too much work? You may be confident you can wing it, but that's like buying a pair of hiking boots for a weekend in the mountains without trying them on. You might get lucky, or you might wind up with a very uncomfortable fit.

You don't have to be an artist to draw an effective floor plan. Accuracy is more important than talent. As you develop your ideas, it's possible that your plans may change. This is why it's worth taking the time to do a basic floor plan at the start.

Assembling the Right Tools

You'll need:

- A carpenter's steel retractable measuring tape with an inch-wide blade. It's accurate because it remains straight when measuring.
- A 60″ plastic or cloth measuring tape. Use for curves and hard-to-measure spots. Cloth may be slightly inaccurate, because it stretches.
- A clear plastic ruler to draw straight lines.
- Pencils, erasers, pens, and colored markers.
- A sketch pad with plain paper.
- Graph paper, preferably 8 1/2″ x 11″, with 1/4″ squares. One square = one foot; one inch = four feet.
- 3/4″-wide masking tape.
  Optional:
- A metal or plastic template called a "French curve," which features both large and small curves for tracing.

■ A furniture template kit, with punch-out shapes and graph paper. (Available at stationery, office supply, and some craft stores.)

Measure Tight and Stay Loose

Before you take any measurements, do the rough floor plan. It's the first step in creating a bird's-eye view of your room.

1. In pencil, loosely sketch the outline of your space on plain white paper. Draw the walls, adding any nooks and crannies.

2. Note doors, doorways, and windows. Mark significant architectural features, especially fireplaces, columns, and built-ins. Walk around your space as you double-check your drawing.

3. Now go back and measure your space with the steel measuring tape, starting with the walls. Jot down measurements on the rough sketch, placing wall measurements just outside the plan's outline. Reach the end of the tape? Just mark your restarting point with a piece of tape or with chalk. If the room is furnished, move lighter things out of the way; get creative (perhaps even acrobatic) with the bigger stuff. No cheating in hard-to-measure spaces!

4. Be sure you've added measurements for all features that affect the shape of the space. Indicate the swing of doors (in or out) with an arc. Don't plan for anything large or important behind a door, and leave adequate clearance.

5. Note the positions of outlets, light switches, TV and computer connections, and phone jacks. Do they seem right for the new plan? When you rearrange a bedroom, you don't want the only phone jack to wind up behind a high dresser.

Floor Plan Symbols

Antenna outlet:
Ceiling fan:
Floor telephone outlet:
Telephone:
Three-way switch: S_3

Electrical outlet: ⊸⚬⚬

Cable TV: (TV)

Computer connection: ◁

Scaling Your Drawing

After the rough sketch comes a floor plan, drawn to scale on graph paper.

1. Draw your walls to scale (work in pencil for this), transferring measurements from your sketch. Use a scale of 1/4 inch = 1 foot. As a reminder, note this scale in the corner of your drawing.

2. Fill in other features, with measurements.

3. Use a plastic ruler to straighten and refine the lines.

4. Add directional orientation, with North at the top. This way, you'll be able to take quality of light into account when choosing window treatments, lighting fixtures, and placement of large plants.

5. Go over walls, windows, and fireplaces with a heavier straight line, either in pencil or pen.

6. Note the inside width of doorways and room openings (arches, passageways, pocket doors, etc.). You'll need these exact measurements when you're moving large items into a room.

7. Make multiple photocopies of the final room plan. You'll use these as you try furniture arrangements, decide on floor and window treatments, and experiment with your new look. Put a set of drawings into your traveling file.

Extra Credit: Elevation Drawings

It's helpful to have an elevation drawing, as well, made to scale. This is a drawing made straight on, facing the wall (or walls) and includes elements from the floor plan. Looking at walls from a standing position is helpful when planning window treatments, deciding on the placement of tall pieces, figuring out furniture arrangements, and "seeing" artwork in place. With a new or total redo, go the extra distance with elevation drawings.

Double-check the measurements of every window or door you intend to treat with new shades or curtains, just to make sure they're exact. Structural variations aren't confined to old houses, so don't trust your eye on this one.

The time you invest in making an accurate floor plan will be rewarded many times over as you move through your decorating adventure. Now with your plan in hand, let's move some furniture!

Simple Math

To figure out a room's square foot measurements, multiply the room's length by its width. A 10' x 14' room has a square footage of 140 square feet. When figuring square footage for an L-shaped (or odd-shaped) room, break up the large space into smaller squares, figure out the square footage of each square, and then add them together for your total.

Arranging Furniture on Paper

Now that you've got your room on paper, it's time to arrange the furniture in miniature. By creating paper models of furniture you have, you can experiment with different arrangements, without straining your back. Frequently, ready-made furniture templates are no more effective than the templates you can make in minutes.

1. Use graph paper with a scale of 1/4 inch = 1 foot.
2. The furniture templates should include all things you own and things you intend to acquire. Sketch furniture and prominent objects in the shape of the piece: round, oval, oblong, square, etc. In the case of an odd-shaped piece, such as a chair or lamp, block out a suitable shape from the piece's measurements. Don't forget to include in your measurements the full flare of the sofa back and the full width of the wings of a wing chair. Even a short finial on a tall clock can make a big difference. Fringe on rugs counts, or your hall runner may run, indeed, out the door.
3. After you've cut out your templates, you may decide you want to work with templates made of paper heavier than graph paper. It's easy to trace the shape of the individual templates onto kraft paper or matte board; even shirt cardboard from the laundry will do. After you've cut out the heavier pieces, be sure to label them.
4. Start playing with furniture arrangements on one of the copies of your final room. I say "playing" because you're free to be adventurous. After all, it's just on paper.

HOW A FEW CHANGES
MAKE A DIFFERENCE

Before: *The framed painting is too small for the wall. Without the tall flower arrangement, this corner of the room would appear blank. The challenge: Fill the wall space effectively and bring the area into better balance.*

During: *A loose rendering (no artistic skills required) of a large painting under consideration is made on brown paper and secured in place with painter's tape. The result: The size and colors of the painting are excellent, the small sofa pillow pointless, and the lampshade looks almost like it is floating in space.*

After: *The oil painting by Maine artist Nance Parker becomes a successful and pleasing addition to the room. The new lampshade is in keeping with the room's bright floral touches, and a fern plant adds a lush accent to the corner. (The little pillow is not missed.)*

Taping Out the Scene

I have trouble "seeing" my dream room on a flat piece of paper. For this reason, I like to use masking tape, heavy brown kraft-type paper, and photos to create a kind of virtual plan on site. Obviously, this is far easier to do when you're working with an unfurnished home space. But the basic idea works for smaller areas as well.

Your Room's Feng Shui

The Chinese art of placement for the maintenance of balance and harmony has caught on in the non-Asian world. Everything from the path to your front door (which should be curved) to the color of your room (red is *the* lucky color) is believed to affect your health, luck, and fortune. Before you work out your furniture arrangement, you might want to find out more about how to use mirrors to redirect *chi* (energy) and why it's good to hang wind chimes.

- **Masking tape:** Measure and tape out the actual height, width, and depth of a piece on the wall and the floor or carpet. Do this for every major piece in the room, including rugs. If you're planning for bookshelves or built-ins, tape out design ideas on the bare wall.
- **Photo:** When you've decided on the place for a standing piece, something that backs up to a wall (cupboard, table, entertainment center), tape a photo to the wall in its place. (Think twice about this method if walls are covered or freshly painted. In any case, use painter's tape, which is easier on surfaces than regular masking tape.) For seating arrangements, I place photos on the floor in position; ditto for rugs and major objects. The "photo method" assists spatially challenged home decorators (like me) to visualize the finished room.
- **Brown paper:** (Use instead of, or along with, the masking tape technique.) Cut brown kraft paper to simulate the width, length, and depth of a piece. Tape it in place. The full-color funnies section of the newspaper makes a great stand-in for a patterned rug.

Elbow-Room Considerations

Virginia interior designer Dee Thornton says arranging furniture is her favorite part of any job. She offers the following guidelines for the amount of space to be allowed between some important furnishing elements.

- Make sure there's from 9 to 18 inches of knee space between a sofa and a coffee table. Less will mean you'll be bumping your knees; more means you'll be reaching.
- Keep passageways between 24 and 36 inches around or behind things. When the room is crowded, you'll notice the difference.

Keep a room's overall design *harmonious by repeating related lines. In a formal dining room, the lyrically curved handle of a pedestal bowl created by Arkansas ceramic artist Gary Eagan and the gentle outline of a Queen Anne–style chair establish a sense of unity.*

- Allow 12 to 18 inches between chairs at a table.
- A desk or a dresser needs 12 to 36 inches of pull-out space for the drawers.
- Dining tables are generally 27 to 29 inches high. Keep at least 6 inches between someone's knee and the underside or apron of the table. Chronic leg-crossers will thank you.
- When you pull back a chair, you need 24 to 36 inches.

From the Design Bible

When you stand in front of your closet and put together an outfit for an important meeting or a special event, your mind is busy evaluating the basic elements of design. Does the red in the tie work with the colors in the suit? Are the heels of the black suede shoes too high to wear with a long skirt, or would you look more put together with dressy boots? As soon as you finished reading the first chapter, you began to relate the same personal design elements to your home.

The basic elements and principles of design that follow should be applied to every decision you make about home aesthetics, be it arranging pictures or doing over the whole place. Your home space will come together more easily, and certainly more successfully.

THE ELEMENTS OF BASIC DESIGN (REQUIRED READING!)

Five important elements make up the theory of artistic design.

Line: Vertical lines can slim, elongate, and heighten. They're dignified and uplifting. Horizontal lines are like the landscape—sweeping, inviting, less formal. Diagonal lines are more dynamic and unexpected. Take care that you don't create distraction with too many of these adventuresome angles. Curved lines are the way of nature: flowing, gentle, restful. It's exciting to incorporate a variety of harmonious lines into your room, letting one play off another. On the other hand, a style in which line is a dominant design factor, such as the straight forms of the Arts and Crafts movement, will reflect that influence.

Color: It establishes mood quicker than any other element. Color is a great magician, too, creating illusions of space, light, and ambience.

Texture: Smooth or sensual? How things feel to the touch provokes a certain ambience. Texture is even more important in neutral rooms, because it adds needed interest.

Mass: You can have mass (or bulk) in one large piece or in a grouping. Mass is determined by actual size and, even more important, by how something *appears* in the room. Too little mass can make a room seem unimportant and "lightweight." Too much mass is oppressive and cumbersome.

Form: This refers to room structure (fixed architectural elements), as well as to furniture and decorative pieces. A traditional rule says that formal rooms call for shapes that are, among other qualities, stately, restrained, and delicate. I believe that it's possible to put a bold, whimsical, or present-day piece in a formal room, if the mix works.

THE PRINCIPLES OF DESIGN

The ultimate goal is to put design theory into practice through a number of easy-to-follow principles.

Focal Points

A focal point is a strong point of interest that draws you into the room and gives your eye a place to pause before it moves around to the rest of the space. Every successful room needs a strong and pleasing focal point. Often, the focal point is an architectural feature—a fireplace, large window with a fabulous view, or graceful French doors. A focal point can be created with prominent or dramatic pieces—an armoire, built-in bookcase, bold painting, even a wonderful tree. (Please, not the TV!) The rest of your pieces will play off the focal point.

Try walking into the rooms of your present space to see where your eye lands. Is there a focal point? Does it please you? If your eye goes directly to a window with a fire escape, an unsightly old radiator, or a dinosaur of a bookcase, note this on your plan.

Balance

Remember getting stuck at the top on the seesaw? That's because the weight of the other kid didn't balance out your side. An unbalanced space is uncomfortable, top-heavy, and overwhelmed by other things in the room. There are two types of balance—symmetrical and asymmetrical.

These relaxed, *asymmetrical mantelpiece arrangements can be great fun to do, or totally frustrating if you try too hard. Keep these tips in mind: Don't crowd, unless that's the look you're after; vary size and height of items displayed; work with an odd number of items for asymmetrical arrangements and an even number for a more formal look; add some bold images or objects that "read" from across the room; and don't forget to add fresh flowers.*

Symmetry is considered formal and traditional. It's about matching, centering, straight lines, working with pairs and even numbers, restraint, dignity. A symmetrical arrangement generally has identical features on both sides of the center (or the design axis) of a room. If you admire historical rooms, find yourself buying pillows that match, and wouldn't be caught dead with the sofa on a diagonal, then a symmetrical arrangement may be perfect for your design sense.

Asymmetry is considered casual and contemporary. Think mixing and matching, alternating, working with threes and odd numbers, arranging things off-center, curves, diagonal lines, informality, and experimentation. Compatible features are arranged on both sides of the center (or the design axis) of a room. Artful mismatching for asymmetrical room design can be slightly more difficult to pull off than an orderly symmetrical arrangement. But if you find yourself arranging three unmatched pitchers on a shelf, mixing plaids and florals, and setting the table with a collection of one-of-a-kind vintage crystal wineglasses, then asymmetrical design may be right for you.

Contrast

Contrast is about varying the elements of design so that they play against one another, thereby heightening the total effect. Contrast can be subtle (tricolor fringe on a plain fabric pillow), or it can call attention to itself (a lemon yellow slipper chair set against a Chinese red wall). Too much contrast is confusing, because your eye doesn't know where to focus; too little can be flat and uninteresting.

Harmony

Harmony is about how the different elements of design have been combined. Play it too safe, and the room is dull. Get carried away, and the room looks forced. Harmony is difficult to pin down; often, it's more a feeling, a sense, or simply knowing that something works.

Rhythm

Composers create memorable works through rhythm and repetition of a theme. In design, the same concept is called the "repeated visual element." Use a favorite color as a repetitive theme: the crimson of a rug pattern repeated in the trim of the sofa pillows, then in a solid fabric for the upholstered side chairs. The repetition of furniture shapes (the curves of a chair repeated in the sensuous lines of a table lamp) can create rhythm, as can themes of collections (folk art, contemporary handblown glass, vintage textiles). So get rhythm!

Furniture Arranging Logic

When I asked interior design expert Dee Thornton for advice about applying these principles from her own experience, she offered a checklist to set your thinking in motion:

- **Have you varied the height of pieces within the room, so that the room is not heavy on one end?** Think of a boat with the entire crew's gear at one end. An unbalanced room feels equally capsizable.

- **Have you used a variety of shapes?** Hard, straight edges need softening with curves, and vice versa. Introducing a square glass coffee table in a room of squishy upholstered pieces can add the edge you need. The shape of accessories counts for a lot.

- **Think about your rugs.** Does the room-size rug fit under the furniture? Do smaller rugs make the area feel cut up? Would wall-to-wall carpeting unify your pieces?

Clueless

When we redesigned a rambling Victorian farmhouse, I assumed the house's maze of hallways, nooks, crannies, and alcoves would be a perfect way to use my antique hooked and woven rugs in combination with Ken's tribal and Oriental designs. Despite compatible design elements, the rug arrangement resembled stepping-stones or, worse, a rug showroom. We wanted to enjoy the old pine floors, so wall-to-wall carpeting was out. It was clear we needed to simplify and unify, so I turned to the principles of design. First, I made sure the spirit of each rug (color, texture, pattern, style) worked in its particular space. Soon, I realized that the unrelenting display of strong design elements needed breathing room. That's when I decided to place natural sisal runners, trimmed with black cloth borders, between the patterned rugs to separate them. (My bordered sisal rugs came from two good catalog sources: Smith + Noble and Pottery Barn.) This broke up the busyness, unified the spaces, and allowed the individual beauties to show off.

- **Is there enough breathing room on both sides of the sofa?** Have you tried placing the sofa on the diagonal for something new? Or considered using two smaller sofas in a conversation area?

- **Wish you had an extra table for special dinner parties, but don't know where to put it?** Consider a traditional drop-leaf table. When the leaves are lowered, a table with a narrow center section becomes a handsome sofa table.

- **Does your furniture face the best direction?** If there's a great view from a picture window, try to take advantage of it. On the other hand, if you like to sleep late but your bedroom faces east, try not to position the bed facing the rising sun. (Or buy blackout shades.)

- **Have you taken the obvious way out by lining up pieces against the wall?** If so, think of ways to take advantage of the space in the center of the room.

- **Are there sufficient pathways, walkways, and spaces for people to move around?**

A Useful Project: You Be the Guest

Pretending you're a guest in your own home, do a mental walk-through of your plan. If you're having tea in the chair by the fireplace, is there a place to set your cup? Can you find your way from the bed to the bathroom in the dark without tripping over a boudoir chair? When you read in the comfortable chair near the window, will the thriving rubber plant behind the chair tap you on the shoulder? Much of smart design is common sense, so be a practical "guest."

Decorating Dilemmas

MIRROR, MIRROR

Q: I'd do a floor plan, but there's not very much floor space in my dollhouse of a home. Is there an instant way to make it look bigger?

A: Try working a bit of magic with mirrors. They can open up a small space, reflect other features of a room, bring a garden scene indoors, brighten a dull room, and reflect candlelight in the most romantic way. Use one wonderful large mirror, or hang an arrangement of smaller mirrors as you would framed artwork. For instant gratification, mirroring can be done on the flat inside panels of shutters, on stair landings, even cut to fit tabletops. If you can't find a mirror to fit the space, choose from the many original frame samples at a store that does custom framing.

7

PUTTING A
PRICE ON STYLE

Final Sale

It's impossible to put a price on style.
However, for practical considerations,
you must bite the bullet and do a budget.

As soon as you have a pleasing floor plan, it's time to do a reality check of your bank account. Spending wisely and effectively is an essential part of home decorating. An overextended budget often results in guilt, high-interest loans, bickering with a partner, or downsizing in the middle of a project. At the other extreme, trying to stretch a modest budget can mean skimping on quality and compromising on taste.

The Unavoidable Budget

Take time now to talk dollars. You'll feel more in control of the total project.

Put the name of your decorating project/room at the top of a blank sheet of paper. List your total available budget at the top and bottom of the page. This number reflects available cash, plus what you intend to pay for on credit. Add a tentative date to begin actual work and a target date for completion. In a wide column to the left of the page, list your decorating purchases and costs in a logical order. Be sure to include:

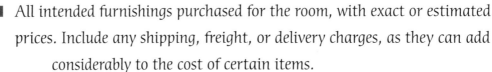

- All intended furnishings purchased for the room, with exact or estimated prices. Include any shipping, freight, or delivery charges, as they can add considerably to the cost of certain items.
- Outside labor and materials (painting, carpeting, window treatments, carpentry, etc.). If installation is not included in the total, make a separate entry for that.
- Cost of redos, such as reupholstering, slipcovers (cost and labor), replacement shades, paint, replacement hardware, etc.

A Sample Budget This sample room budget may help you plan for what works best for you.

Sample Home Decorating Budget Worksheet

Project/Room: Living room

Projected Budget (amount you have put away or are comfortable borrowing
   or charging): $_____

Projected Start Date: _____

Target Completion Date: _____

ITEM and/or LABOR	Estimated Cost	Actual Cost
Painter		
Paint and supplies		
Artist fee to paint trompe l'oeil scene		
Paperhanger		
Wall coverings and supplies		
Carpeting: antique Oriental rug		
Built-in shelving for stereo and objects		
Design/plan		
Carpenter labor and supplies		
Painting (if extra)		
Electrician		
Move two outlets		
Install ceiling fan		
Ceiling fan		
Lighting		
Replace two ceiling fixtures		
Purchase brass floor lamp		
Sofa		
Slipcovers for two existing club chairs		
Labor		
Cost of fabric		
Three lined linen Roman shades		
Plants and their accessories		
Ficus tree		
Decorative pot for ficus		
Two needlepoint pillows (use Mom's needlework)		
Labor and materials		
Trimming, backing, zippers, goose-down inserts		
Total Costs as of _____ **=**		
25% Cushion =		
Projected Budget =		
Difference =		

Sometimes, the simplest solutions *are the best, as well as the most cost-effective. Dark-stained paneling in a bedroom, or any other space that needs a bright lift, can be painted. With this single change, everything else in the room looks new and refreshingly different.*

How Much Is that Lampshade in the Window?

- ■ If you need to come up with ballpark figures, check Web sites, catalogs, and furniture stores.
- ■ Start saving your favorite catalogs (a useful and current Resources section listing mail order and Internet shopping is included in the back of this book).
- ■ Ask friends and neighbors to recommend reliable painters, carpenters, refinishers, and other skilled trade professionals. Often, retail home-oriented stores keep a list of outside freelance companies and individuals. Some community bulletin boards provide a place for business cards, so check there. And, always, ask for references.
- ■ Be sure to get estimates, and get them in writing.
- ■ Unless you've worked with someone previously, get at least two estimates and compare. If there's an enormous spread, either the quality will be radically different or somebody's padded the estimate, so ask questions.
- ■ Go for the best quality you can afford.

Playing It Safe

At the end of the project, total up the actual bills and compare them with your estimate. As a rule, the final tally comes in higher (especially with forgotten shipping, taxes, and your lunch at IKEA), so add an overrun cushion (the pros suggest 25 percent) to keep your budget in line.

Singing the Over-Budget Blues

There's no need to abandon your dream look if your budget comes in higher than your plan allows for. Prioritize your needs, and decide on a realistic amount you can spend. Some of your project can probably wait. Put a permanent treatment for walls, windows, and floors at the top of your list for a good foundation. Remember that a lasting look evolves. Instant decorating is for set designers.

Smart Ways to Cut Costs

Find yourself in a cash crunch? Is your wish list looking unobtainable? Get savvy by discovering clever ways to improve your purchasing power, as well as things you can do in stages.

- Look for established furniture stores that offer professional help or discounts for ordering above a certain amount. If your purchases include furniture beyond one or two pieces, develop a relationship with your favorite store's interior design consultant for advice and to be notified in advance of sales and special offers. Ask if there's a minimum purchase amount required to qualify for the store's design services. Make sure the sales and design personnel understand that you don't want to be locked into one source—unless a particular store is your one-stop shopping dream come true.

- If you're into "finds," check out the various trade secrets books. Shopping in New York City? Pick up Tracie Rozhon's *The Cheapskate Millionaire's Guide to Bargain Hunting in the Big Apple.* Tracie turns you on to designer fabric and wall coverings at cut-rate prices, lampshades that are always on sale, spots for wonderful odds-and-ends trimmings, and other smart, cheap shopping. For sources outside of New York, look at the back of decorating magazines. Travel and in-flight magazines are also good sources of shopping information. If the listed sources are too rich for your budget, window-shop for ideas.

The most cost-saving treatment *may be no treatment at all! If the windows don't require covering for privacy, light control, or camouflage, leave them unadorned to open up any space in a pleasantly airy way. Bare wood flooring is a friendly surface that can either be covered with rugs or carpeting at a later date or left plain and simple.*

- Install simple and inexpensive blinds or shades until you can invest in more costly window treatments. Home Depot sells pleated paper shades (a serene Oriental feeling) in standard sizes that are fixed to window trim with Velcro®. Bed Bath & Beyond sells inexpensive, heavy fabric shades. Canvas and sailcloth fabrics in a dark color make excellent blackout shades as well. Of course, the other option is to leave attractive windows refreshingly bare.

- Search out do-it-yourself frame shops that stock standard sizes of framing materials. Sometimes a shop is set up so that you can do your own framing on the premises.

- If your ideal is color, color, color and your budget is tight, paint one room gloriously. Keep the other rooms neutral, bringing on the color in stages. The more you change paint color, the more the cost of your paint job escalates.

- When using different colors throughout your home, use the same trim color in all of the rooms. This works for cost cutting as well as for design continuity.

- Find suitable transitional pieces until you can invest in your ideal.
- Explore flea markets and antique malls for unusual finds. The Rose Bowl in Los Angeles is the site of a famous flea market, where celebrities can be spotted among the finds. Or schedule a fun

Virtual Antique Shows

The Internet is a great place to track down antique shows. *Maine Antique Digest* (www.maineantiquedigest.com) provides a full calendar of shows with numerous links. But don't just click on the calendar; enjoy the entire site. When I last surfed for outdoor antique markets, I came across www.scottantiquemarket.com, a wonderfully personal and chatty site devoted mostly to shows in Georgia. It made me want to go just to check out the Victorian walnut drawer pulls.

weekend at one of the sprawling outdoor antique shows, such as Renningers near Lancaster, Pennsylvania. A newly married couple, preferring furniture with a past for their new place, rented a truck and headed for a regularly scheduled outdoor antiques extravaganza held in Brimfield, Massachusetts. They swept through two hundred acres of antiques and "junque." Working with a modest budget, the couple managed to furnish their first apartment with tasteful and unusual finds. Many such shows are announced in magazines and newsletters dedicated to antiques and historical restoration.

Useful Project: Playing with Numbers

Prepare a budget for your decoration project, again making sure to leave yourself a cushion for cost overruns. If you aren't decorating right now, make up a budget for an imaginary redo.

Decorating Dilemmas

A GREAT STAND-IN

Q: Our goal is to buy antique Oriental rugs for our main rooms, but we can only afford to start out with one and then add rugs over time. In the meantime, can you suggest something nice, neutral, yet reasonably priced in floor covering?

A: If you're looking for suitable stand-ins for good antique Oriental rugs, consider a reasonably priced natural sisal area rug (wool sisal runs somewhat higher). It's a great clean look, and one that goes with just about any style. A neutral rug allows furnishings to stand out. If that's too plain a look for you, have a simple rug trimmed with a wide decorative border, solid or patterned, that picks up the room's colors.

8 SETTING THE STAGE
WITH COLOR AND
TEXTURE

sky blue

china blue

bluebird

blue denim

cornflower blue

blueberry

baby blue

blue delft

Dealing with the Blues

Glorious color! It's everywhere, and it's the first thing you notice when you enter a room. Even the drabbest room has color—the mellow tone of pine floorboards, a book's cover, the red Japanese maple outside the window. Color establishes a mood, one that shifts to cool by moonlight and warms by the glow of the sun. Strong color associations—your lavender prom dress, the jalopy you painted an outrageous red—stick for a lifetime. Some of us crave vivid color contrasts, while others long for hues that whisper. It's a mistake to let your color choices go along with the ho-hum crowd or, at the other extreme, mimic the latest trend. If you paint your bedroom the color of a valentine, it may affect your mood at midnight, but can you face that jolt of "red passionata" before your morning coffee? You want colors to be livable and be *you*.

Innovation in Color

For one of his designer showhouse room creations, noted designer T. Keller Donovan framed groupings of paint chips in colors compatible with an orange-and-white room. This memorable artwork, in warm reds, yellows, apricots, peaches, and pinks, cost very little and continues to be talked about (and copied). Relish the same variety as you search for colors that work with a sublime dusty mauve, a formal statement in blue, the bold orange of a New Mexico sunset, or a sassy turquoise that talks back.

Prioritize Color

In her lavish and eye-opening photographic book *Color,* design writer Terry Trucco says, "Combining colors with imagination, style and wit is one of the toughest challenges confronting anyone who designs a room. Fortunately, the payoff is worth any struggle along the way."

When decorating, you need to keep in mind a color scheme, in which each color bears some relation to the others. Fabric, carpeting, furniture, accessories—even painted picture frames— need to possess harmonious hues, their different values and intensities having some relationship to the others. Make color a priority. Your mood depends on it.

A pop of color *in the right place is all it takes to create an effect. A vividly painted wall has become a kind of stage curtain to introduce the next room with a sense of drama not possible with beige or white.*

Color Basics

It's time to start giving the painter directions more specific than "Well, it just doesn't look like the blue I picked out!" Know the important terms and components of color theory and you'll communicate more clearly.

When you were a kid and art class was your favorite period, do you remember how magical it

Social Faux Pas in Living Color

The story my husband tells about buying a suit on sale for the first important social event of his fledgling investment-banking career is, among other things, a bittersweet color lesson. Eager to impress his seniors, Ken went suit shopping on a very tight budget at one of the old guard men's stores in Baltimore. I'm sure he looked dashing as he stood before a mirror in the store's elegant red-carpeted fitting room, wearing a well-cut herringbone suit in pleasing shades of maroon (considered a distinguished color for business suits at that time). The night of the event, Ken took the new suit from its signature garment bag to dress for success. But when he stood in front of his bedroom mirror, it appeared that the suit had transformed itself from a subtle maroon to a far brighter color, with a distinct leaning toward red. A red suit definitely was not the color of success, at least not in Ken's line of work! Had the store pulled a switch? Hardly. In the store's fitting room, the suit color had been changed visually by its surroundings, toned down by rich red carpeting, mellow wood-paneled walls, plus the lack of natural light. Feeling more like Bozo the Clown than a hotshot young executive on the move, Ken wore the flashy suit that night, since it was the only dress suit he owned. The following week, the store exchanged the infamous suit for something more bankerlike.

seemed when you mixed blue and yellow for the very first time? As you review how color is organized into groups, you'll find joyful, new color surprises.

Primary colors: Red, yellow, and blue. These colors are pure, unmixed. All other colors are made from mixing them.

Secondary colors: Orange, green, purple. To create these colors, two primary colors are mixed in equal parts.

Tertiary (or inter-mediate) colors: Blue, green, yellow-green, yellow-orange, red-orange, red-purple, purple-blue. To create these colors, one primary and one secondary color are mixed in equal parts.

Colors are changed visually by their neighboring colors. An armchair, upholstered in a lively periwinkle blue, sits against a clean white wall. Place that same blue chair in a yellow room, and (much like your childhood experiments with mixing colors) the chair will appear slightly green. Always check color selections against each other. Be sure to factor in the color's value (the brilliance or luminosity) and saturation (the penetration or depth), as well as the amount of natural light in the room.

Most home decorators don't shop with a color wheel, which is a circular diagram that contains a rainbow of precisely arranged colors. Used most often by people involved in design and the arts, the color wheel is a tool for determining colors that work together, or don't. In the end, however, most design professionals let their eyes tell them what works. After all, some of the most unpredictable combinations become decorating news.

Color Roundup

Black: Some think chic, others think sorrow. Black absorbs light, so take care when using it in larger areas, and consider additional lighting. Fabulous as an accent.

White: Fresh and peaceful. White reflects light, so rooms seem larger and brighter. When color becomes frenetic, calm things down with white. Turn to an ivory for a soft, pleasing, and elegant look.

Gray: An easy-to-live-with neutral; popular for modern tastes. Too much can come off as too plain. If you savor gray chic, add drama with a splash of bold color (orange silk pillows on a gray flannel sofa).

Red: Red is an energetic color—as an accent or regal background. Its very presence sends messages: *Stop! Look this way! I'm bold and I know it!* Be sure to try red before you buy red.

Orange: It's Halloween in April unless you proceed carefully with the pure hue. Consider soft melon or peach with a touch of yellow. Orange adds energy to a lackluster space.

Yellow: A longtime favorite, yellow warms and cheers. Use it pure to sunny up children's rooms, kitchens, family areas. Use its creamier cousins for a flattering glow.

Green: It's associated with bounty and nature. Visualize the spring green of new buds, the lush green of midsummer, and the golden green of autumn. Adds intensity to a room, or tones it down.

Blue: There's navy blue for order and truth; sky blue for calm; turquoise for punch. An appealing accessorizing color—as in blue English Staffordshire china, blue Depression glass, Picasso's "blue period."

Purple: At one extreme, a noble color; at the other, difficult and risky. People seem surprised and delighted when purple works, as it does in our bedroom (soft mauve walls) juxtaposed with apple green walls in the adjacent bathroom (plum purple and drab green towels). Just remember that light changes purple in dramatic ways.

The simplest and most effective way *to add interest to the objects on a shelf is to paint the back of the shelf with contrasting color. In this case, a plain white bookcase (above left) gets a jolt of color. With two coats of a zippy raspberry-colored paint (above), the small and interesting items on the shelves come together.*

Colorspeak

Color is expressed through a variety of terms.

Neutral colors: Black, white, gray, and brown.

Color temperature: The degree of hotness or coldness of a color, expressed as warm, hot, cool, or cold. Light has a particular temperature as well. It can go from a warm yellow on a sunny morning to cool gray on an overcast day.

Warm colors: Colors found on the red side of the color wheel: red, orange, yellow. Think intimate, intense, highly saturated, enlivening. Taken to warm extremes, you have the hot colors, which are stimulating, zesty, bold.

Cool colors: Colors on the blue side of the color wheel: blue, violet, certain greens. Think reserved, soothing, calming, proper. Taken to cool extremes, you have cold colors, which are somber, static, and sometimes depressing when used without relief.

Hue: A particular color's family name, such as red. The hue is further defined with a descriptive name, such as "poppy red" or "sage green." If you need to describe an exact color to someone (a painter or a salesperson), relate it to something that's relatively free from color variations: marigold orange, parsley green, robin's-egg blue, paper-bag brown. Describing more unusual colors requires a sample: a paint chip, a magazine clipping, a scrap of fabric, or a piece of colored ribbon.

Color value: The degree of lightness or darkness of a color.

Color intensity (tone or chroma): The brightness of a color.

Tint: Colors closer to white in value.

Shade: Colors closer to black in value.

Yuck!

When my daughter was four, I took her with me to a show of huge paintings done by an abstract artist. As we stood among a reverent crowd of gallery-goers, Erica took one look at a particular painting and declared loudly: "Too much green!" Total strangers smiled and nodded, possibly because she was right. You don't want to feel this way about the color of your living room walls. Try out that color before you're crying the blues or the greens.

The texture and daring green color *of this wall might well be located in the south of France rather than on the New York shore. Walls can be given dynamic visual texture with a variety of painting techniques.*

Color Schemes and Strategies

The following questions are meant to help you decide how you intend to use color to shape your rooms.

- Do you long for a room that's white-on-white? Or is white the perfect backdrop for all the bright furniture in your life? Bo Niles's classic photographic book *White by Design* explores the many looks of white.

The Five Hundred Colors

When design writer Terry Trucco moved into a new apartment, she was torn in several color directions, so she opted for cream-colored walls throughout. She used the vivid colors she loved as lively accents.

Terry was hunting for a jazzy color touch for her living room when she stumbled across an enormous display box of colored pencils, on sale in one of her favorite art stores. Measuring 5 1/2' x 2', the box contained five hundred sharp bright pencils. Terry bought it on the spot. Set atop a low bookcase, this truly unusual color find succeeds in pulling together all the colors of the space.

- Color can be used to create optical illusions. Bring one wall closer by using a darker color, or push it away with a lighter color. A dark color on the ceiling in a low room will turn it into a canopy.

- Uneasy about using hot tangerine? Start out by using it as a bold accent color, and take it from there. Decorating is more exciting when you take a few chances.

- How will the room's light conditions affect your color choices? The quality of available natural light changes by the season, by the climate, by the minute. Factor in that aspect.

- Will color be the main attraction of your room? Or will a solid or more neutral color become a backdrop for other things (photos, art, collections, antiques)?

- Having trouble narrowing down the fantastic choices? Relax. There's no color finish line.

Color Scheme Possibilities

There are three general color schemes:

- **Monochromatic scheme:** This scheme uses tints and shades of a single color. Think blues, ranging from periwinkle to navy. Tone-on-tone refers to a single color with a low intensity in a limited range of values. Avoid monotony by adding an accent with a bright color—long-stemmed lilies in an emerald green vase, flannel throw pillows in red-and-black checks, colorful and graphic artwork.

- **Related (analogous) scheme:** Features neighboring colors that blend well, plus combinations of those colors. For example, blue with purple and with purple-blue. Used to create a calm atmosphere.

Arrest That Woman!

I like the push-pull effect of contrasting colors and patterns, and our apartment's loft space includes soft vintage colors (rose, burgundy, green, yellow, wispy blue), played against intense shades of green, red, and rusty orange, and punctuated by black. The colors mix it up in solids, checks, plaids, stars, and florals. There are no "color stars," though there are strong focal points, including an abstract painting on the most prominent wall, which, not surprisingly, incorporates most of my favorite colors.

To avoid overkill, I've kept the background simple and neutral—white walls with a touch of yellow, white fabric shades, a large sunny arched window left bare to its pleasant bones. It's better for me when I allow a color scheme to evolve.

■ **Complementary (contrasting) scheme:** Features contrasting colors, such as blue and orange. Used to create a lively atmosphere.

Steps to Color Harmony

There are seven million colors perceptible to the human eye. How in the world does anyone decide on just one? Here's one way to start:

■ Decide on your main colors.

■ Decide on your secondary, or accent, colors.

■ Preview samples of every color in the room on your sample board. Play with the pieces of your color collage till they look harmonious and balanced.

Elusive Texture

Texture: Its qualities are subtle, like the wool sofa fabric you didn't really notice until midsummer, when your legs were bare. Texture is tempting, mysterious, sensual. What happens when you spot a sign that says, DO NOT TOUCH? Are you tempted to brush against the velvet dress on display at a store, or run your hand along the cool curve of a bronze statue?

Designers and fiber artisans may crush pieces of velvet in their hand and say, "It has a good hand." They're talking about a textile's thickness, richness, quality, and stability—in short, the way it *feels.* Someone's personal response to texture varies. A mohair throw feels soft and cozy in the depths of winter, but what will it feel like in muggy July?

More than you realize, texture is an everyday, everywhere occurrence.

■ *Rough* emery boards

■ *Smooth* silk pillowcases

■ *Coarse* straw hats

■ *Soft* furry slippers on a cold morning

Too often, texture is overlooked. A room without texture lacks dimension. Incorporated into a decorating plan, texture adds interest, balance, and harmony. If you can't pin down what your room lacks, look for texture.

See It, Feel It, Sense It

Exactly what is texture? Everything can be said to have texture, tactile or visual. You're familiar with all the adjectives, such as nubby, hard, coarse, smooth, soft. Surface interest is another decorating term for texture. The way light reflects off surfaces is sometimes referred to as "visual texture." Pattern may also be called "visual texture."

■ Shiny, glossy, luminous surfaces (lacquered tables, mirrors, glass, some pottery) reflect light and add movement.

■ Dull, matte, rough surfaces (dark flat paint, unfinished woods, grass wall covering, carpeting) absorb light, adding shadows and depth.

The Texture of Home

Become more aware of the texture in your life. Make a list of things with significant texture in one room of your house.

■ Texture is found in the bones and basic features of the place, as well as in decorative accents: a stainless steel counter, a marble floor, stucco walls, exposed wooden beams, brick walls, a pressed tin ceiling.

■ Texture can be three-dimensional (sculpture, objects).

■ Texture can be found in relief on flat surfaces (carved panels, decorative molding).

■ Line produces texture. An arched doorway pulls eyes away from poor walls; the squares of the floor tile set up a textural pattern for the room. Furniture and accessories have clear lines that create formal (straight) and informal (curvilinear) texture.

When you start looking, you'll be amazed at how important texture is in your surroundings. If you need a quick texture fix for a monotonous room, there are inexpensive and easy solutions, including baskets, dried flowers, wooden bowls, and earthy pottery for rustic environments; small mirrors, silk pillows, glass vases, and bone china in more formal spaces.

Using strong color accents, *such as this hot pink wicker table in a black-and-white country bathroom, provides warmth, charm, and surprise. If color is used only once, make sure the object or piece is oozing with character or charm, as it will stand out.*

Working with Texture

Explore rich and exciting ways to work texture into your plan.

- **Consider texture's message.** More often than not, rough surfaces say casual and rustic (a cabin with a twig chandelier and leather furniture), because they hold light and make shadows. Smooth surfaces tend to say contemporary and formal (a streamlined room with mirrors, silk upholstery, and polished floors). Their ethereal moods are created by reflected light.

- **If you decide to have texture as background, consider a wall covering, such as grass paper, moiré, or suede.** Be creative. A young artist on a shoestring budget covered the walls of his one-room apartment with corrugated cardboard, rippled side out. It hid poor walls and made his shabby furniture look more earthy.

- **Surprise people with sharply contrasting textures.** Juxtapose smooth with rough (a sleek glass vase on a weathered barn wood table); shiny with dull (a rustic painted bench sitting on a highly polished floor). You'll call more attention to *both* features this way.

Sensually Speaking

During the years when everyone felt the need for lots of chintz, I decided to slipcover my sofa in a bold rose-patterned chintz fabric, its crisp glazed surface perfect for a summer look. But once my cool sample had become a large slipcover, my English country vision looked more like plastic. My once comfortable sofa had turned unyielding. Trying not to think of how much I'd spent on this little venture, I checked the care instructions of the fabric—luckily, 100 percent cotton. So I tossed the slipcovers into the washing machine, set the dial to "cold," and held my breath. Line-dried and pressed, the stiff finish was history and my slipcovers looked and felt pleasantly timeworn. Postscript: Try this with chintz fabric at your own risk!

- **Don't neglect the texture found in small decorative details.** These include fringes, trimmings on pillows and upholstery, metal trim on furniture, carpet borders, and so on.

- **Avoid going overboard with textural contrast, especially in smaller spaces and with rugs.** A long-haired Greek flokati rug tends to dominate the space, as do shag rugs. Not only do we notice them, but we also sense their rich texture when we walk on them. Extreme textures do have their place, but choose carefully.

- **For more unity, avoid sharp contrasts.** Many modern styles make a more dramatic impact with sleek and shiny surfaces.

Camera! Action!

Take along a camera when you shop (also, a 25-foot steel measuring tape). If color, texture, or patterns are prominent elements and samples aren't available, move in for a close shot. You won't have a perfect match, but it will help you remember the shade of green or the distinct cut of the pile. Don't forget to jot down the measurements for easy reference.

If you own a color printer, you can print out shopping photos from the Internet of rugs, fabrics, artwork, or any decorative feature that's shown in a large format. The color matches will not be altogether true to the real thing, but this gives you the general idea of how the item might look with the other colors and designs in the room.

A Useful Project: Chips, Anyone?

Find a friendly paint store—that is, one that doesn't count the number of paint samples you select. Stroll through the color possibilities as though you were in an art gallery. Clear your mind of decorating plans, and then select colors that you adore. Be spontaneous, impulsive. Fan out your selections on a table, assorted according to hue. Do your colors harmonize? By trusting your color instinct, did you choose colors that work together? If not, pull out your favorite chip and find other chips that make the selections look more harmonious. In this way, you'll expand your vision of color gradually. By the way, this method works well with fabric choices, too.

Choosing color with a partner? Select colors separately, and then compare. If your selections look like Monet's garden and your partner's like the American flag, remember that countless color combinations are found in the same flower garden. Usually, dividing up the rooms between partners ("Now you take the color of the bedroom and I'll take the color of the family room") comes off as disconnected.

A courtesy note: The paint store thanks you for putting back any paint samples you won't be using.

Decorating Dilemmas

READING COLOR SAMPLES

Q: Many paint samples contain three or four colors to a strip. How do you "read" a paint strip? Am I missing something?

A: When I spoke with Lesley Merritt, an independent dealer for Benjamin Moore Paints, she said that her own company had started to arrange their color strips from light to dark, using paint colors that contain the same colorants. "This seems to be the system many paint companies are going with, but be sure to ask the dealer or sales staff before you make this assumption," Lesley told me. This useful system means that you can combine the colors shown on the same strip in the same area without worrying that they won't work together. Naturally, it's a different matter when you're matching different colors by eye, using only one color, or using the colors of a particular collection. By the way, if your color of choice is white, Benjamin Moore offers the Off-White Color Collection, containing more than 140 different whites. That mind-boggling fact should keep the white-on-white fans busy.

9

COVERING
THE WALLS

Be Creative

Unless you live in a glass house, it's hard to ignore them. One of the first things you need to do is to decide how to cover the walls—hence, the category of "wall covering." This category is a catchall for techniques from paint and traditional wallpapers to wall decor of a less predictable nature, such as plaster applied over fine wire mesh for a textural effect.

About Paint Types and Finishes

Hands down, paint is the most popular method of handling wall surfaces. Often, a fresh coat of white paint, chosen from the countless variations of white, does the trick. Possessions stand out against this clean canvas. If you're a color person, the shades and tints of orange alone run from a wisp of peach to a bold harvest orange. Both paint colors have the power to transform a room. But before you buy one pint or ten gallons, expand your paint savvy with essential information. The two readily available types of paint are:

Oil-based paint (also called alkyd):	Takes longer to dry than water-based paints; the strong smell of petroleum distillates requires good ventilation; recommended for damp areas; adheres to a variety of surfaces, such as wood and metal. Thin with paint thinner or turpentine. Many people swear by its durable finish.
Water-based paint (also called latex):	Dries quickly, with little or no odor; applies easily with a brush or a roller. Latex paint can be thinned with water; easy cleanup with soap and water.

"Paint finish" refers to the level of sheen—a little or a lot. The higher the sheen, the more imperfections are revealed. Your basic choices are:

Flat (or matte):	No gloss; forgiving finish on walls with flaws
Eggshell:	Slightly more sheen than flat; can be washed
Pearl:	More sheen than eggshell, but very subtle
Satin:	Lowest gloss; recommended for wood trim
High-gloss:	A hard, glossy surface; durable, but flaws become obvious

The word "enamel" refers to highly durable paints containing certain properties that allow

When shopping for furniture, *remember that pieces painted in a shiny finish will reflect light and open up the whole space. The look is rarely limiting, as painted furniture is wonderfully compatible with traditional finishes. Who could resist jumping onto such a pleasing bed?*

them to be washable. (Not to be confused with a glassy substance called enamel, which is fused to metal and pottery.)

Painterly Tips

■ The shinier the paint, the more light reflection and "lift" you can expect. Flat paints absorb light and appear softer.

■ The better paints can be costly, but many so-called bargains contain fillers (such as talcum), and sometimes they fail to cover adequately and to last. A good paint's smooth and easy coverage alone can make up the cost difference.

■ Most paint stores can match a particular color by using a special computer technique. The only thing you need to bring is a large enough sample (a flake of the color may not do it), whether it's a favorite red silk blouse or a sample from the discontinued color you used last time.

■ Paint that is mixed according to your specifications is called "custom-mixed paint," as opposed to premixed paint, and the extra cost may be worth it. Ask the paint store to provide a fully dried color swatch of any custom-mixed paint for your inspection.

Good Wall Prep a Must!

Without proper wall preparation, even the finest brand of primer and finish coat will be doomed from the start. The requirements for wall prep escalate with its condition and the type of paint finish. You've got fix-it options, including a wash-down, light sanding, taping of heavy cracks, spackling over rough spots with a plastery substance called "joint compound," and more sanding. Stores such as Home Depot and Lowe's stock helpful how-to books and manuals, not to mention materials and supplies. In the past, paint contained lead, a harmful substance, especially if ingested by children. Lead-based paint used in older buildings should be removed. Your health depends on it.

No Time to Spackle?

No interest in improving your landlord's space and your temporary digs? Go with a flat finish. Into "crumbling chic"? Scrape off loose plaster, then spackle roughly, going over the entire wall in casual patches. Looking for a clever ruse? Once, to buy time before a renovation, I painted my flaking plaster walls a rich chocolate brown, then replaced dark fabrics—bedding, diaphanous curtains, slipcovers for a chaise—with pristine all-white, with a splash of pastel hues provided by a handwoven rug. This fresh and dramatic contrast drew eyes away from background imperfections.

Decorative Painting Techniques

Faux finish: In this decorative paint category, nothing is what it seems. *Faux* is French for "false." Is it tortoise, bamboo, leather, wood grain, or exquisitely veined marble? If you must look twice or touch the finish to be sure, then the impression is a deftly created illusion. The term for a fake wood finish is *"faux bois."* A fake marble finish is *"faux marbre."*

Trompe l'oeil: This French term means, literally, "to fool the eye." It's a specific area of faux finishes. Generally, the term "trompe l'oeil" is used to describe photo-realistic painted scenes—antiquarian books begging to be leafed through; a pet cat on a fence caught midyawn. A word to the wise: Truly convincing faux and trompe l'oeil work is best left to the experts, or the truly artistic. There's a big difference between a lovely rendering of a rose bouquet and wanting to touch the petals to see if the bouquet is real.

Stenciling: This is in a category all its own, with many levels of effect and complexity. Start with a simple stenciled border, or a scattering of stars above a window.

Gilding and silvering: These are elegant ways to give wall trim an upscale glow. There are specially designed paints that add a romantic shimmer of gold or silver. These metallic finishes may be rolled on, hand-rubbed, dry-brushed, or dabbed onto newly painted walls and woodwork. First, experiment on a piece of Sheetrock or board that is painted with your wall color. Prepackaged metallic-finish kits are springing up faster than goldenrod.

Lacquering: This is a sophisticated glasslike finish, simplified greatly since its origins in ancient China. Today, lacquered walls are most frequently obtained with paint. Executed by experts, walls take on unequaled luminosity. But it's a tricky process that, if not done well, could resemble the uneven work of a third-rate auto body shop. If you're yearning for the glamour of lacquer, a highly finished coffee table might be more realistic and within the reach of the average budget.

Other decorative finishes: The possibilities are exciting. With *sponging, spattering,* and *ragging,* you're only a paint kit or a how-to video away from success. Other techniques, such as *feather painting* and *combing,* require more practice, or the hand of a pro. Luckily, the names of the various finishes are also the revealing names of the techniques or materials used to achieve them. *Color-washing* and *glazing* are two more techniques, both within the scope of the home decorator.

Wallpaper's Rich Variety

Design archives across America are filled with treasured wallpaper motifs from the past, with many styles carried into today's perfect reproductions. Variations on old themes turn up as fresh revisions. Innovative contemporary wallpaper breaks new ground, taking its place in the visual tour of textile history.

Given the rich heritage of design, why is it that one look at any wallpaper store's stacks of gigantic sample books sends the fainthearted fleeing to the paint department to order plain and simple "designer white"? Take your time with wallpaper. Begin by exploring the many possibilities, then narrow down your choices to design motifs that speak to you, as you envision a particular space.

Wallpaper Talk

Wallpaper has descriptive categories and specific terms. The following lists contain examples intended to help you to develop a more specific wallpaper language.

Place the pattern in a major category.

- Plain
- Textured
- Damask
- Geometric
- Architectural
- Floral
- Abstract
- Figurative

Determine the style or period description.

- Traditional and updated traditional
- Contemporary
- Classical
- Historical period paper
- Faux finish effects

Decide on a motif.

- Exotic trees
- Leaf designs
- Wildlife
- Vintage florals from the thirties
- Bouquets

Narrow down scale, background, and arrangement.

- Large-scale, bold
- Miniprint, small-scale, diminutive
- Plain ground
- Pinstriped background
- Open, scattered
- Dense, overall
- Diagonal

Consider the color scheme.

- Blues only
- Tomato red
- Muted
- Monochromatic
- Contrasty
- Bubblegum colors

Pinpoint an aspect important to you.

- Scrubbable
- Reasonably priced
- Prepasted
- Easy to work with
- New and different

Use descriptive everyday words.

- Playful, whimsical
- Cozy, cheerful
- Romantic, dreamy
- Formal, elegant
- Earthy, natural
- Simple, clean, spare
- Cool, sleek

Something New

It's possible to create a striped wallpaper effect with paint, assuming your walls are straight enough for this treatment. If you're planning for a wide yellow-and-white striped design (wide stripes are easier to work with, as are light color combinations), apply the lighter paint color (in this case, the white) to the entire wall. When the paint is completely dry, mask off wide striped areas with painter's tape, which comes in a variety of widths. It's important to measure carefully and be precise. The exposed areas will receive the yellow paint. When the tape is peeled off (very carefully) the striped effect will have been created.

Interior designer Dee Thornton offers a truly novel technique for painting stripes on walls. This time, only one color of paint is used for all the stripes; however, the bands of color are alternated between a satin finish of the color and a flat finish of the same color. Instead of reading as a solid wall, Dee says the wall takes on a rather magical and subtle effect.

Wallpaper Types

There are two main types of wallpapers:

Hand-screened: These are hand-printed. Often richly colored and distinctive, they are costly, usually untrimmed, and rarely prepasted.

Machine-printed: There are countless choices at affordable prices. The washable papers are coated with a plastic film; the vinyls are thicker and scrubbable.

Border Ideas

Many wallpapers have coordinating borders, which really stand out when used with solid-colored walls. Take care that your borders don't make the room too overly "done," too "mixy matchy," or too cute for words. Architectural-motif borders are stylish accents; they add character to rooms having little or no wood trim, often fooling the eye. Use paper borders with other wallpaper, with paint, and on smooth, decoratively painted walls. A border affects a lower ceiling, or fills in for an absence of crown molding. In a small kitchen or bathroom, borders add charm, without closing in the space. They act as substitutes for chair rails and as window trim. However, a border is effective only when there's a logical reason to add it. Never use a border just for the sake of having a border you happen to adore.

A child's room *is a great place to have fun with wall surfaces, especially if it's a utilitarian loft space such as the one in the photograph. The pajama-clad ballerina has a length of jazzy fabric to display her artwork and souvenirs, and bold crisscross images alongside the fabric point to a creative homemade "wallpaper" project.*

Other Wall Covering Options

■ Think about using fabric, from burlap to velvet. But first, consider a fabric covering's suitability to the space and your life. (Jellied hands and stretching cats don't go well with gray felt.) Consider the room's natural light. A fading chair can be moved away from the sunny window, but a wall covering has to take the heat. Applying fabric to walls can be tricky and frequently requires professional application. Despite the obvious drawbacks, a fabric look on walls can be truly elegant and inviting. Heavy fabric wall covering cuts down on street traffic

and loud voices, and cozies up a space, especially if the decorative fabric is applied over an upholsterylike wall padding.

■ Large mirrors, hung or affixed to the wall, can open up a space or reflect a room's positive features. Take care when mirroring large walls though, especially in rooms where you spend a lot of time. Even the most extreme narcissist must tire of looking in mirrors.

■ If you're into novelty treatments, try draping fish netting from the crown molding, wallpapering with old *New Yorker* covers, or hanging large workout mats on the walls of a sports-loving teenager's room.

Brown-Bagging It

A sensational and cheap alternative to traditional wallpaper comes in the form of brown kraft paper, the heavy kind used for shopping bags and wrapping paper and widely available at craft and home improvement stores. It can provide a serene backdrop. Set it off against simple white trim for a Zen-like look.

Although I do love the look, I've yet to try it. A painter or your local paint store should be able to come up with good technical advice.

Playing Safe

Sometimes, even professional paperhangers get it wrong—measuring for wallpaper, that is. I know, because I have enough leftover rolls from a whole-house decorating job to paper the Washington Monument!

■ Begin by taking a careful measurement of the walls to be treated, arriving at the total square footage (see "Simple Math" in Chapter Six). Take this number, plus a sketch of how the room's wall space is broken up, to a salesperson or paperhanger, who can pin down the number of rolls you need.

■ The amount of wallpaper needed is also based on the width and length of a roll (European and American measurements differ) and the way any pattern repeats itself in the design (logically called the "repeat"), which figures into accurate matching. If you're thinking of wallpapering on your own, consider asking a friend to help out. The prepasted papers are easier, but a first-rate application of any wallpaper is a tricky and physically demanding job.

- If you're making a special trip to a wallpaper store or a wallpaper outlet, usually it pays to order all the wallpaper at once.

A Useful Project: Reflection

Make a list of the words you'd choose to use if you bordered a room with personal thoughts or sayings. Think of a lyrical word with a thought-provoking sense ("serendipity"), or a lively quotation ("Approach love and cooking with reckless abandon"). Even if your words never make it into wall art, the project may turn into a wonderful time for reflection.

Decorating Dilemmas

DIZZY WITH CHOICES

Q: I've decided to do all three bedrooms in wallpaper, because I like the inviting tone wallpaper sets. But I'm having trouble making up my mind. Surrounded by so many patterns in a wallpaper department, I get dizzy and frustrated, and don't know which way to turn or which book to open. How can I become more efficient in narrowing down choices and finding the right design? Wallpaper doesn't just pull off.

A: You're right that wallpaper has the ability to establish the tone of an entire room. And that it's not easily removed. If you choose bold daisies, when you should have opted for stripes, the error surrounds you daily. And, yes, with so many possible choices, even the most experienced shopper experiences overload.

That's why the majority of wallpaper manufacturers and distributors offer handsome sample books of designs, with wallpapers especially suited to particular rooms and moods. You'll find everything from "Kitchen Inspirations" to "Romantic Bedrooms."

10

COVERING

THE FLOORS

Rug Illusion

Look down! Floor covering can make a tremendous difference to the design and feel of any room, not to mention its ability to muffle the downstairs neighbor's new woofers. But the many choices on the market can confuse even the most experienced interior designer. There are two types of flooring: hard surface and soft surface. If you consider these treatments in orderly categories, it's easier to get a handle on the subject.

Hard Surfaces

Logically, "hard surface" refers to any flooring that is not carpeting.

Synthetic and/or resilient flooring: Practical and highly attractive materials (including linoleum, cork, and vinyl in tile and sheet forms) provide a range of do-it-yourself possibilities.

Stone and/or hard flooring: Includes the fabulous, and often costly, brick, marble, granite, stone, slate, glass blocks, and a wide variety of tiles, from terra-cotta to porcelain, as well as concrete, which can be dressed up with paint, tints, and other finishes. I advise using a stonemason for this complex type of home construction project.

Wood flooring: This encompasses soft wood (most pines) or hardwood (oak and cherry). Few home decorators lay their own wood floors. Some feel more confident about sanding a preexisting floor and applying various decorative techniques, like staining, pickling, and stenciling.

JAZZING UP OR TONING DOWN WOOD FLOORS

Pickling: A transparent film adds a color cast to raw wood (choose from a variety of pickling colors, such as cream white, soft gray, and pale lime green). This technique brings out the grain's textural beauty. If your floors have been dark, the lighter, softer finish (color-washed in appearance) makes any room look surprisingly airy.

Liming: Liming is another way to highlight the grain of the raw wood. It's similar in effect to pickling, but this time a pigment is rubbed into the grain of the wood. This technique can be used in a formal or a rustic way. Woods are distinctive, so heart pine is going to give you a different effect from a grainy oak or a light ash.

Wood flooring *lends itself to a variety of decorative treatments, among them staining, pickling, liming, stenciling, and, of course, painting. Be open to the many options, as every floor has different requirements and possibilities.*

Staining: Go darker or go lighter. A stain chart shows your many options. Deep, rich stains add drama and a more serious quality to a room. Light stains open up spaces in need of an airy quality. A high sheen will reflect light; a low sheen will soak it up.

Stenciling: Your artistic technique need not be limited to walls and objects. A stenciling style works wonders as a floor border, an allover design, or to call attention to a small or odd-shaped area, where anything short of a custom-cut rug is impossible. Do stenciling over stained, painted, limed, or pickled floors. Use one or many colors.

Painting: Porch paint is durable and available in a variety of colors. White is clean; black is smart; orange is playful. Looking for the unusual? Do a glorious Jackson Pollock–style floor by spattering, swirling, and dripping. First, practice on a large sheet of primed plywood board and experiment with techniques and color combinations.

Soft Surfaces

If it's softness you want underfoot, look first to the wide world of carpeting. Carpeting is considered flooring because it generally covers an entire floor space. Area rugs cover a large section of the floor. Rugs cover smaller areas.

MACHINE-MADE CARPETING

Machine-made carpeting is divided into residential and commercial grades. Commercial grade does not necessarily refer to the boring beige carpeting at your office. Its durability and cleanup ease, combined with the many stylish patterns and textures, often make commercial grade the best choice for your home. It tends to be slightly more expensive, but should pay off in durability.

Following is a glossary of terms relating to machine-made carpeting, which will help you shop knowledgeably:

Bonded carpet: Fibers are heat-bonded to an adhesive backing.

Broadloom: Carpeting woven on a wide loom; generally, 9-, 12-, 15-, and 18-foot widths.

Fiber: The material content. Natural fiber (wool, cotton, sisal), synthetic fiber (nylon, polyester), or a combination (blend).

Gauge: Indicates the amount of space between stitches. Lower numbers indicate a tighter weave.

Pattern: Can be printed, dyed, or woven- or tufted-in.

Pile: The rug's surface, which can be cut (velvet is an easy cut pile to remember) or looped (uncut), or a combination of the two techniques. Depth of pile ranges from shallow to deep. Looped pile has a tendency to unravel, making this pile every cat's first choice.

Runner: Commercial carpet is sold in widths of 6 feet, which is cut to fit your space. It can be cut to any length.

Sample: A representative piece marked on the back with certain manufacturing specifications, including (but not limited to) fiber content and country of origin.

Stitch count: Higher numbers mean that more yarns were used per square inch, hence, a stronger carpet.

Synthetic dyes: The most common type of dye and more reasonably priced; colorfast, but less subtle than vegetable dyes.

Tufted carpet: Tufts of yarn are punched by needle (not woven) into a backing (often jute), which is then sealed with adhesive before a second backing (often a cushioned material) is added.

Vegetable dyes: Derived from plants and insects; natural looking; important to the wonderfully muted look of antique Oriental rugs, which are highly durable but subject to fading.

Woven carpet: Loops of yarn are run in a continuous fashion from front to back; done on a loom, with threads interlaced, creating a very strong carpet.

CHECKERBOARD FLOOR

Bonded carpeting is available in tile sizes, usually sold by the box in one color only. If you come across a sale of individual tiles in a rainbow of colors, consider creating a playful checked carpet wall-to-wall in a game room or space that craves a touch of whimsy. Or alternate black and red for a person-size checkerboard.

HANDMADE RUGS

Handmade rugs run the gamut from brightly colored American cotton rag rugs to Tibetan wools in subtle tones and designs. Oriental rugs (antique carpets as well as reproductions) are part of an ancient weaving tradition, passed along through generations. Handmade rugs fall into a number of categories:

Hand loomed: A popular form of rug weaving today, it dates back to Colonial America, when rag rugs were woven with colorful cotton scraps from the "rag bag." Other examples of woven rugs include the flat-weave Native-American Navajo rugs, the nomadic kilims (flat-woven to be pliable enough to roll and carry on the back of your camel), and dhurries, some of which reverse for a double life. Many of the older hand-loomed rugs were made with natural vegetable dyes. The softly muted colors are easy to use in home design, but many of the natural dyes run on contact with spills or pet stains.

Knotted: This is a method used for genuine Oriental and Persian rugs. Yarns are tied and knotted, one at a time; then knots are cut off or left knotted. The more knots per inch, the more valuable the rug can be. Fine antique rugs are treasured textiles.

Hooked: Cut strands of yarn are hooked through a coarse backing, forming a floral, geometric, or pictorial pattern; often thought to be too good to walk on, so elevated to wall art, especially the antique textiles; cat motifs are coveted. The abundance of lovely and expressive rugs from modest Prince Edward Island, Canada, is attributed in jest to the length and severity of the winters there.

Braided: Strips of wool, cotton, and synthetic materials are braided; sometimes made with novelty materials, such as plastic bread liners, women's stockings, and men's ties. These rugs are round, oval, and heart-shaped (charming for hanging on a wall).

Needlepoint: Wool or silk yarns are carefully stitched in and out of a mesh (usually canvas) backing, often stamped with a design for the amateur needle-worker to follow. Popular motifs include pets (especially dogs), flowers, and copies of beloved quilt patterns.

An interesting choice for small areas is floor cloth—a piece of painter's canvas cut to rug size, turned under around the edges and affixed, then decoratively painted, and, finally, sealed for durability.

BUYING HANDMADE RUGS

When buying from dealers and specialty shops be sure to:

- Ask a lot of questions about the rug, the region it comes from, its age, and, if of recent vintage, the reputation of the weaver.

- Ask about the rug's fiber content. If it contains synthetic yarn, it can't be that old.

- If the rug is an antique Oriental, look at the size of the knots on the back. In general, the smaller the knots and the higher the number of knots per inch, the more expertly the rug is made. However, this is not the sole gauge in rating the value of a rug. A good dealer imparts to a potential buyer a range of knowledge on the complex subject.

A Lesson Learned About Antique Orientals

A fine antique Oriental rug is a true investment that comes with a fascinating and complex history. Some years ago, I signed up for a lecture course on Oriental rugs, offered by a New York auction house the month before every major rug auction. My minicourse was a terrific hands-on experience and attending the lively auction was hardly "homework." I was fortunate enough to be living in a large city, where auction houses are a great place to explore the world of rugs and other textiles. There are many informative books on the subject, including *Oriental Carpets: A Complete Guide* by Murray L. Eiland. This total guide is wonderfully oversized and thorough, and features more than three hundred large photographs.

- Ask about colorfastness and durability, especially if you own a pet. The vegetable dyes in my wonderful dhurrie rug ran faster than my excitable new puppy.
- Get laundering or cleaning instructions. Ask for recommendations of rug cleaners.

If you're interested in learning more about the history and styles of older rugs, there's a long list waiting at your local bookstore or through on-line sources. I continue to enjoy the reliable sources on my shelves, including *American Hooked and Sewn Rugs: Folk Art Underfoot* by Joel and Kate Kopp.

The Shape of Things

Traditional design advice is: "Start with the rug." Although this is no longer carved in stone, it's important to appreciate the valid reasoning behind the advice, especially when it comes to the *dimensions* and *shape* of a room, and how much of the floor space you plan to cover or leave bare.

A wall-to-wall treatment provides an overall canvas. Both the color and the style of the carpeting should harmonize with things you own already. If you're decorating with a brand-new look, first make sure you're happy with the total design scheme, and then order wall-to-wall carpeting. Don't make the mistake of saying: "Oh, that neutral will go with everything!" And then, when the new sofa arrives, find out that you were wrong. Many home decorators prefer to work the color, pattern, and texture of a rug into the overall design scheme of a room at a later date, especially if the floor covering of choice is a combination of area rugs and smaller rugs. This makes sense, because most people like being able to rearrange the rugs with the furniture. Don't limit your ability to do this.

Artist Brad Stephens's *one-of-a-kind living room holds his own folk art creations, as well as art and accessories acquired over many years. The individual pieces stand out smartly against solid-colored upholstered furniture, a rich wall color, and neutral carpeting.*

Making Changes from the Floor Up

Whatever your plan of action, many of the same elements and principles of good design are applicable to carpeting and rugs.

- Use flooring to change the visual shape of your room. A boring square room can be broken up into areas—conversation areas, recreation areas, passageways, and "islands" where tables are set. A long room may look like a corridor with wall-to-wall carpeting. By breaking up a long space with a large central rug and area rugs placed at the ends, your eye reads three defined spaces.

- Runners establish pathways and lead people in a certain direction.

- If you want to set off a nook or a cranny, place an interesting rug there.

- A rug with lengthwise stripes will make a space seem longer. Stripes that run from side to side take your eye in the same direction, visually widening the space.

- Remember that the end of a rug says "stop!" Continuous carpeting or a series of connected area rugs beckons the walker to "keep going."
- A round rug is much like a friendly round table; it brings people (and furniture) together.

Carpet and Rug Buying Tips

First, consider the *function* and *practical needs* of your floor covering. Will it be purely decorative? Will it function as soundproofing for a child's room or insulation for your new sound system? Do you want something soft underfoot when you get out of bed in the morning? Do you work, read magazines, or watch TV on the floor?

Here are some tips to think about:

- On a tight budget? A plain rug, bordered with a solid-color fabric tape, is a smart and simple buy. Also, it has the ability to unify the furniture arrangement.
- To liven up a plain rug, or add yet another coordinating pattern to the room, choose from a myriad of decorative borders for the rug—tapestries, floral prints, animal designs.
- If a solid-color wool rug is a custom order, ask about having a wide border made lighter or darker to "frame" the rug.
- Many rug manufacturers offer plain sisal rugs, decorated with colorful stenciled designs, painted scenes, and other decorative painted touches. If you adore creative projects, your plain rug could become a one-of-a-kind, with your own signature on the back.
- Room-size natural-material rugs, such as those made of sisal and grass, make pleasant backgrounds—however, be aware that these materials often stretch (especially wall-to-wall) and stain instantly. Consider commercial-grade wool sisal, which does a good job of mimicking natural sisal in color and style. Plus, it's easier underfoot.
- Handmade and decorative rugs can "float" like floor art when placed on top of wall-to-wall carpeting. A somewhat permanent method of tacking with heavy thread is recommended. (This type of sewing is not recommended for the occasional seamstress.) Generally, the undercarpeting needs to have a flat low pile, as the double thickness could be an invitation to tripping.
- The right rug can turn into a focal point. The rug's design can say: formal, casual, ethnic, playful, elegant, or happily neutral.

Cruising the Net for a Bargain

Whenever I shop for a rug, my upper arm muscles get a workout on the colossal display hangers, which have a tendency to push you around. To make matters worse, all the rugs I want to see are located, without fail, at the bottom of the heaviest piles. I apologize profusely to the floor employees, who flip the enormous rugs like hot pancakes. So I was thrilled when I discovered a stress-free way to shop for just about anything: on the Internet. Not buying necessarily, but narrowing down the choices. (Successful on-line shoppers tend to go to sources and sites they know and trust, and they make certain they have full return privileges.)

The genuine desire to find a rug for the bedroom motivated me. I did a search with words that would narrow down my choices: "area rugs + floral + wool." When a dizzying number of sites popped onto my screen, I went to familiar names first. If the site's merchandise mix didn't click with me right away, I went to another site.

During my second excursions with Web rug shopping, I discovered my match at www.capel-rugs.com, the site for Capel, Inc. Using a color printer, I produced large images of a number of favorites in the right size. The color images provided me with a close enough sample to determine if my final choices worked with other patterns and colors in the room. The nearest Capel outlet was a modest drive away, so I hit the road. In the end, I bought a lovely floral-patterned wool rug at the outlet, a style very similar to one of my Web favorites. It was well within my budget, plus I had approval privileges, just in case. My Internet rug shopping was an eye-opening experience—a process with a stylish outcome.

■ When I owned a home furnishings retail shop in New York City, I sold handwoven cotton throw rugs, which customers said they liked to use in front of the kitchen sink. Find a pretty rug that's colorfast, one you can toss in the washing machine on a delicate wash cycle. Any rug that needs professional cleaning doesn't belong in a kitchen. An exception to this rule is my own personal choice for kitchens—antique Oriental rugs. An odd choice? Not really, for many Orientals, old or newly made, are absolute workhorses when it comes to durability and resisting stains. They were made to last hundreds of years, and they live up to their reputation.

Essential Rug Padding

Proper padding is a must. A good pad keeps a rug (and you) from slipping, protects it, cushions underfoot, insulates, and extends the life of the rug. Fiber padding (backed with a hard rubber that won't disintegrate) is my first choice for area rugs. For my own small area rugs and handmade rugs, I've discovered a substantial smooth-coated and ventilated polyester rug liner, available from Plow & Hearth (see Resources). It's 3/16" thick, and is available in larger sizes, which I cut to fit smaller rugs. Some of the thin, hard rubber pads are durable and easy to trim, but they stick to floor surfaces, shred, and stretch.

A Useful Project: Considering Your Options

Make a rough floor plan of one room, and then work out at least three different treatments of soft flooring in that room. Your first plan should show wall-to-wall carpeting; the next, a large area rug. Finally, combine an area rug with smaller rugs. Keep the furniture in a fixed arrangement.

Which floor treatment seems best for the space? For the furniture plan?

Decorating Dilemmas

A FACE-LIFT FOR TILE?

Q: Is it possible to paint over old tile? The kitchen tile in my house is dark and unattractive. (I didn't choose it.)

A: This answer is given by Jill Herbers, the author of a comprehensive book on the subject entitled *Tile,* which has just been reissued in paperback. Jill says: "I'm afraid that painting old tile will prove to be disappointing. Tile is an organic material, made from the earth and fired to its final state, and is meant to remain that way. It's better to install new tile, or cover up old tile with carpeting, or even put a beautiful rug over old tile. If most of the floor area is covered, the old tile won't have such an effect. Of course, installing new tile is the best option, but be prepared that good tile will be an investment. If you choose wisely, your tile will last a lifetime, and longer. Choose classic tile, such as terra-cotta squares, especially if you change decorating styles every few years. Terra-cotta goes with anything, from country to the modernism of black leather and chrome pieces."

THE POSSIBILITIES OF FABRIC

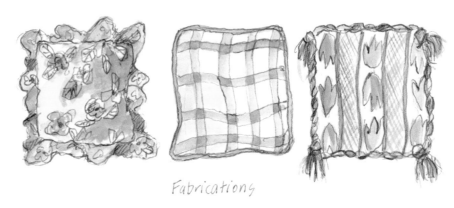

Fabrications

On a softer note, it's time to shop for fabric. For many of us, it's the reward for working so hard on a budget and a floor plan. But before you lose yourself among large-scale banana leaves and a textured maroon silk fit for royalty, take a moment to consider the role of fabric in your total decorating scheme.

Plain (Solids) and Patterned Fabrics

Plain fabric:

Also referred to as "solids," it is a name given to the fabric group that has no trace of pattern. Solids run the gamut from the wildly colorful to shades of white. Many people opt for solids because they think they won't tire of them as quickly. But a too-cheery yellow can wear thin, and a boring solid beige won't last as long as a timeless beige print. Anyway, change is good for the spirit, which is why someone tossed a sheet over a chair and invented slipcovers.

Patterned fabric: It embellishes your furnishings and adds interest to your surroundings. Pattern is the repetition of a distinctive design element: the red-and-black striped tie that gives you the perfect "power" look; the vintage floral tablecloth you snapped up at a garage sale—they're examples of our pattern-filled lives. Frequently, intangible patterns in our lives go relatively unnoticed: the orderly arrangement of louvers on your closet door, or the rich grain of your dining table.

Pattern Basics

Patterns in home furnishings fabric and wallpaper fall into easy-to-remember categories. Often, you'll find them arranged this way:

- **Geometrics:** Contains geometric shapes.
- **Florals:** Featuring representations of flowers.
- **Figuratives:** Containing identifiable subjects other than florals, arranged in a motif, or repeated design; includes novelty prints.
- **Abstracts:** Patterns devoid of a representative form.

Historically Correct

Many of today's patterns are taken from patterns of the past. Pattern design in Colonial America arrived with the Pilgrims, packed in trunks and in memory. Fabric archives collect examples of old fabric and wallpaper, and today we can enjoy the identical charming calicos and straightforward ticking patterns, faithfully reproduced or stunningly updated.

Taste in historical pattern ranges from Greek urns to the stunning Arts and Crafts nature motifs of William Morris, from a Western cowboy design to Victorian posies. If you'd like to know more, look up *Period Style* by Mary Gilliatt, a succinctly written book with lavish photographs.

Selecting the Right Pattern

Vintage Memories

During the 1980s, when odd yardage of vintage floral fabric began making a comeback at flea markets and in the jam-packed vans of country dealers, I was won over. The timeless designs, so softly and freely rendered, appealed to me far more than the current hard-edged floral designs. Oversized hydrangeas, printed on textured cotton, as well as lush peonies on a trellised background, made the loveliest slipcovers and pillows. As I filled my home and my retail shop with vintage floral motifs, something felt all too familiar.

Many months later, I was rummaging through an old family album, when I unearthed a childhood photo of myself: little Patsy seated in a high-backed armchair, the chair fabric covered with oversized flowers and elegant arches. It was a fabric that I might have bought the day before and called "vintage." It seems that I'd tucked away this lovely childhood association like a bolt of treasured fabric.

The fabric patterns, or motifs, you choose become an enduring expression of your personal style. Your goal is to find pattern statements that look great for the long term—unlike that leopard-print suit you wore one time.

- Patterns can change the mood of a space. Does your low ceiling need the lift of long curtains with a vertical motif? Will your delicate love seat look ill-at-ease wearing calico, but be smashing in elegant damask?

- New patterns should work with the things you already own. Vivid weavings from Mexico probably won't look right in a restrained Federal-style scheme.

Compatible colors *and patterns pull this room together. The comfortable club chairs and ottoman are upholstered in a pleasing floral design. They stand out against a well-matched orange sisal rug bordered with a diminutive pattern. The wallpaper, with its soft taupe-and-beige colorway, picks up the colors of the flowers in the chair fabric.*

- Use pattern to carry out a theme in one room, and then repeat it in other rooms for continuity, harmony, and rhythm.
- Fabric sample books and ads show rooms chock-full of combinations, all professionally styled and often quite effective. Keep in mind that the goal here is sales. In real life, you may be overwhelmed (or underwhelmed) by a prepackaged look. When you spot a perfect needlepoint pillow in a specialty shop that has a no-returns policy, ask if you can take the item home on approval for a fixed period of time. Many specialty shops extend this courtesy.
- Remember that colors, designs, and patterns that please your eye are reflections of what you like. Rooms that are "done" often look and feel too perfect.

Mixing and Matching

The design approach known as "mixing and matching" is one of the most challenging aspects of home design. Meri Stevens, former president of Waverly Fabrics and current design director for the most recent Laura Ashley collection, suggests that the first step is to select a "statement" print. She goes on to explain: "Whether you use this main print for curtains that sweep the floor, or slipcover one chair with it, your statement print becomes the 'road map' for your other fabric decisions." Meri advises tying a "coordinating" print into the statement print. Of course, stripes and plaids are naturals for that needed variety. "Then go on to select a third 'accent' print to work with the other two," Meri continues. "Differ the sizes, textures, and colors, but keep the look harmonious. Then you can introduce successful new patterns into your established scheme."

Understand the Fine Print of Fabric Language

Plain (or solid): This includes everything from pure cotton with a colorful kick to wool, often more neutral and serene.

Patterned: Also expressed as fabric "prints." A fabric's print can be machine-printed (the affordable majority) or hand-printed (these range from "more expensive" to "out of sight"). Also, pattern can be woven right into the fabric. This fabric type is often referred to as a "weave." Traditional paisley (usually found today as a printed reproduction) is a woven fabric. Fabric patterns may be broken down further according to the size of the pattern (from miniprint to overscale, or oversized) or a characteristic design element (vining, bordered, architectural, etc.).

Surface: A particular feel and look such as smooth, shiny (glazed), or rough.

Weight: Fabrics can be lightweight, medium-weight, and heavyweight. Many of the heavier-weight fabrics are suitable, and more durable, as furniture coverings, so expect to come across the term "upholstery weight." Often, sheer fabric is grouped in its own category, due to this diaphanous fabric's popularity for window treatments.

Please Repeat the Repeat

Many patterned fabrics have a repeat, which refers to how often the entire design repeats itself, as expressed in inches. Yardage requirements for fabrication projects (such as pillows, slipcovers, and window treatments) are dependent on the size of the repeat. Otherwise, the seamstress, tailor, or home decorator may lack sufficient fabric to match up the design.

When measuring fabrics that have a pattern pressed permanently into a solid or plain ground, such as matelassé, consider them in the prints category, as, quite often, the pattern contains a repeat.

What's It Made Of?

Fabric is either natural (pure organic fiber content) or synthetic (any fiber not from a natural source; a product of technology).

Natural fibers:

- Cotton
- Linen
- Wool
- Silk

Synthetic fibers:

- Acrylic
- Nylon
- Olefin
- Polyester
- Acetate

"Blend" refers to a combination of natural fibers and synthetics.

A Note About Synthetics

In the recent past, most synthetics were shiny, scratchy, and, well, just plain cheesy. But vast changes have taken place. Many of today's pure synthetics reveal fresh and innovative patterns, but, better yet, they offer unique qualities, such as being wrinkleproof, fadeproof, and stainproof, which can't be matched in natural fibers. Pure natural fiber blended with a percentage of synthetic fiber can make a fabric more soil resistant, colorfast, and less prone to wrinkling.

The next time you go clothes shopping, check the fabric content, but only after you've tried on the piece. I continue to be amazed that a "silk" dress is really 100 percent synthetic, and my favorite winter trousers are synthetic wolves in sheep's clothing.

Treasure Hunt

My hunting and gathering instincts tell me that a drop-dead mauve silk awaits me in a dark corner of a discount fabric store for a rock-bottom price. On Manhattan's Lower East Side, I'm prepared for adventure. In a warehouse setting, I move aside fabric that blocks the narrow aisles. I leap over logjams of flannels in order to get to a cumbersome roll of a divine brocade, which I drag to a window for a closer look. I check carefully for an irregular lot (seconds), and pray that I won't find a flaw in the yardage I need. In the end, I may come away a winner. Or, I'm still in search of the elusive silk.

If you're ready for such a shopping adventure, make sure you go with the right mind-set. It's not for the faint of heart.

Fabrications

How do you find that perfect fabric? And where do you begin?

- Begin with a stroll through a national retail fabric chain, such as Calico Corners, Laura Ashley, or Jo-Ann Fabrics, to survey the many choices. Many regional areas have their own fabric stores, such as the East Coast's Printer's Alley stores. Don't overlook a solo operation for helpful one-stop shopping. A personal favorite of mine is the Williams & Sherrill store in Richmond, Virginia.

- Many design operations, especially the smaller ones, have more sample books than lengths of sample fabric on display. When you find your perfect fabric in a sample book, jot down the name of the book, the page, the fabric's name, and a brief description (color, scale, width, price). Then request a sample.

- If you know the manufacturer, pattern name, design number, and any other relevant information about your fabric of choice, it's possible to search fabric sites on the Internet to track down your yardage, often at excellent prices. If you're in the market to spend a good bit more for European designers' fabric lines, try www.findafabric.com, a British-based on-line store. Be sure to request a sample before you make a purchase. This site offers a currency conversion, which is very helpful.

■ Be hands-on with fabric. It falls into folds a certain way; it holds or resists creases; it allows light to show through, or not. Handling the fabric, as well as holding it up to the light, will acquaint you with its subtle qualities.

■ Usually, home design magazines list sources for fabrics (and other furnishings) in the Resources section in the back of the magazine. If you see something you like, don't clip the page without making note of any information provided. It's a smart idea to take notice of certain manufacturers and designers you're drawn to, such as Ralph Lauren, Laura Ashley, Raymond Waites, and Waverly. Generally, the colors in their collections are likely to work well together.

■ Trade showrooms usually display large samples of fabric and wallpaper on hanging panels, called "swingers." Always ask for a cutting or a swatch to keep in your workbook files. Make sure the necessary identification for each swatch is attached with a tag, or taped to the back.

A Glossary of Popular Home Furnishings Fabrics

Bouclé: Nubby wool, made up of curly, looped yarns. Elegant yet cozy.

Brocade: A raised pattern, woven with the same thread, creating a subtle light and shadow effect. Effective for upholstery and draperies.

Burlap: A coarse fabric, made from jute, hemp, or cotton. Rustic, informal.

Calico: Characterized by small patterns on cotton; an American country statement.

Chambray: Plain weave with a colored cotton warp (the lengthwise threads on a loom) and a white cotton weft (the threads that cross the warp). Especially popular in blue for bedding.

Chenille: The word is French for "caterpillar," which explains the interesting texture in the fabric's unique pile. Your grandmother's cotton chenille bedspreads have made a comeback for bedding and cozy bathrobes.

Chintz: Also known as polished or glazed cotton, this fabric is coated with a waxy finish, giving it a high sheen; strongly associated with an English country look.

Corduroy: The easy-to-identify cotton pile runs in vertical lines and comes in solids, as well as prints.

Cotton: An all-time favorite, cotton is made from the fiber of the cotton plant and is available in a wide variety of weights, textures, and finishes.

Damask: Similar to brocade, in that it's made on a Jacquard loom, but cotton and silk damasks have a flatter pattern. The fabric is named for Damascus, a city known for its finely woven cloth.

Denim: It's not just your old blue jeans, but more universal; available in a variety of weights and colors. Prewashed cotton denims are more casual choices.

Duck: Also known as canvas (the heaviest weight of cotton duck) and sailcloth (the lighter weight). Nineteenth-century ships' sails were made of canvas, which carried the trademark of a duck.

Flannel: Wool or cotton with a slight nap (fuzzy surface).

Gingham: Dyed cotton yarn woven into stripes, checks, and plaids.

Lace: An ornamental fabric in an open weave.

Linen: Made from the fibers of the flax plant, pure linen is durable, with a slightly rough texture.

Matelassé: A quilted-texture cotton, lovely for bed coverings. The word is French for "padded."

Moiré: The distinctive watermark pattern on ribbed fabric, made by engraving rollers that press the design into cotton, silk, or rayon.

Muslin: This plain-weave cotton includes gauze, mosquito netting, and scrim. The tighter weaves are good for upholstery lining.

Organdy: A fine-thin cotton fabric, with a durable crisp finish.

Percale: A popular sheeting fabric, this is a closely woven cotton (or cotton blend) with a smooth, nonglossy finish.

Poplin: A plain fabric, usually cotton, with a slight weft rib.

Without incurring the cost of a new sofa, *anyone can slip their upholstered furniture into something more comfortable, exciting, or totally different. The striped slipcovers in the photograph replaced dated crushed-velvet upholstery, stained over time by spilled juice and dirty paws. Pillows made of an inviting vintage floral pattern add to the fresh appeal.*

Satin: This can be a silk fabric, a cotton fabric (called sateen), or a synthetic. The look is high in sheen and reflects the light.

Scrim: A cotton or linen with an open weave.

Silk: Dating back as far as 2500 B.C., pure silk is an elegant and lustrous fabric made from a fiber produced by the silkworm. Though it appears delicate, silk is actually the strongest of the natural fabrics. Silk faille and silk shantung (in which the natural knots and lumps are heavenly imperfections) make stylish choices for domestic use.

Taffeta: A crisp, shiny fabric, traditionally silk, but also available in more reasonably priced synthetics.

Tapestry: Woven on a Jacquard loom, this fabric shows strong patterns (florals, historical scenes) to mimic the handwoven silk tapestries of the past.

Ticking: A heavy twill once used to cover mattresses; today this serviceable cotton fabric has gone upscale.

Toile: Dating to the 1700s in Jouy-en-Josas, France, this traditional printed cotton fabric features delightful pictorial scenes of country life, usually in a single color on a white or cream ground. Traditional colors include blue, green, and red.

Twill: A tight diagonal weave of heavy duck; its surface is often brushed lightly (brushed twill). A popular casual look in cotton.

Union cloth: A blend of cotton and linen, usually floral or striped.

Velour: A smooth, dense velvetlike pile that is more durable and less formal than classic cotton velvet.

Velvet: The soft, dense warp pile of this woven cotton, silk, or blend fabric is cut flat or left in its original loop form. Velvet is available in embossed, crushed, or patterned designs.

Voile: A sheer fabric, frequently cotton, whose ability to filter light makes it especially effective for a diaphanous curtain look. Its surface finishes range from a crisp plain weave to a wiry twist.

Wool: A natural fiber, sheared from the coats of sheep, goats (cashmere, mohair), llamas, camels, alpacas, or vicuñas. It comes in its natural shades, as well as a rainbow of dyed colors.

Slipcovering Revisited

Gone are the days when having slipcovers meant the upholstered piece beneath it was tattered or badly dated. Today's formfitting slipcovers and loose furniture covers make a dramatic style statement as well. The many advantages of slipcovers make clear why they've become more popular than ever before.

HEADING STYLES

A heading is a pleating or gathering at the top of each panel.

Pleating: Often made with drapery tape, which has been designed to hold metal pleating hooks. Styles include: box, pinch, goblet, cartridge, and pencil.

Gathering: Often used with a concealed rod. Styles include: plain, gathered, smocked, double-hemmed, and cased.

Rod revealed: A flat panel on a revealed rod; can be pierced and tabbed.

TOPPING STYLES

The topping is the wide horizontal band across the top of the window treatment, which can adorn the window or cover unattractive hardware.

Flat topping: Cornice (also, pelmet) is a hard strip of board, decorated with paint or fabric. A valance is a soft fabric topping. A lambrequin is a three-sided cornice.

Drape style: Swag, cascade, jabot, crossover.

Shade Talk

The other window treatment category is called "window covering." Fabric is an important element in many of these categories, which include:

- Shades
- Shutters
- Blinds

Choosing shades is a way to give any window privacy and beauty, with or without curtains. The old-fashioned pull-up shades, minus any sign of a window treatment, usually meant you'd just moved in or you couldn't afford curtains. Today, shades are an inviting choice.

SHADES

Pull-up shade: The simple roller style is made of fabric and wood, as well as other materials such as vinyl and light-filtering (solar) material. More elaborate fabric pull-up shades include: Roman (pulls up into soft horizontal pleats), Austrian (similar to Roman, except swags remain on

Wood shutters *can offer an architectural accent that soft treatments do not. They're durable as well as flexible, especially where style is concerned. Furniture with simple lines, such as this dining room table and chairs, become almost Zen-like when paired with a floor-to-ceiling window treatment of shutters.*

the bottom when closed), balloon (fuller, with more shirring), and festoon (fancy permanent gathered swags, even when closed).

Down-up shade: Operates from bottom, or center, to top.

Simulated fabric shade: Includes cellular, honeycomb, or pleated.

Tie shade: Rolled and tied by hand.

SHUTTERS

Louver: Fixed or movable; louver shutters with slats that open and close are called "plantation louvers."

Raised panel: Interior panel made of solid wood.

Sash: Interior panel made of fabric, screening, paper, or synthetic material.

- Cookie cutters
- Demitasse cups and saucers (mix and match different patterns)
- Dollhouse furniture
- Doorstops (unadorned or painted iron)
- Fans
- Flower frogs (crystal or pottery)
- Hair combs
- Handbags
- "Junque" jewelry
- Ladies' gloves
- Matchbooks
- Old mortars and pestles (once used to grind spices and drugs in apothecary shops)
- Paperweights
- Pincushions
- Pitchers

Certain objects were meant for fun, *as well as function and decorative appeal. These jars made by Virginia potter Heather White Schott show a bit of whimsy and invite people to smile.*

- Radios
- Rubber ducks
- Tea towels in vintage patterns
- Tin soldiers
- Tools
- Toy trains
- Trivets
- Whirligigs
- Wire whisks

Be as eccentric as you please. In fact, a few of my all-time favorites include:

- A department store brassiere display form from a bygone time (The one I own might be described as a wire torso with breasts. I've elevated my rather curvaceous white wire model to wall sculpture.)
- Clock faces, the decorative old ones
- Glass insulators (once used on utility lines, usually green)
- Pencil sharpeners (a mix of old and new)
- Windmill weights (used for balance)

Nature offers decorative objects for the taking. Consider:

- Beach glass
- Birds' eggs
- Birds' nests
- Feathers
- Fossils
- Gemstones and crystals
- Pinecones
- Seashells
- Walking sticks

Who would have dreamt *that old Indian clubs, used in turn-of-the-century gymnasiums as standard muscle-building equipment, would become "hot" collectibles and spectacular folk sculpture? If you apply vision and imagination, you might find the next new collectible closer to home than you know.*

The Walkabout

Do you have to stand on a chair to appreciate the carving on a primitive whirligig because it sits on a high shelf? Is the impact of an elaborate silver mirror lost against a yellow wall? No doubt the frame and the folk art piece would benefit from more effective placement. But unless you're visually adept, it's difficult to *see* a decorative piece in new surroundings without putting it there.

Enter the Walkabout, my decorating eye-opener for considering new and better marriages of pieces and places. Think of this as a movable feast, when you carry the piece in question throughout every room, hallway, nook, and cranny. Place it here and place it there. Try a ledge, a windowsill, a mantel, a footstool, and the floor. If you come up empty on existing display areas, consider the purchase of a wall shelf, pedestal, or corner cupboard.

Maybe you've been collecting McCoy pottery at tag sales since you picked up a piece for less than a dollar. Over the years, you've set the pieces anywhere you found the space. However, items in collections are far more effective when displayed together. So do a Walkabout with a representative sampling of McCoy pieces. You may find that your full collection rates its own built-in shelving. After all, your tag sale finds have become objects of some value.

The venturesome Walkabout has worked wonders for me, with objects as well as with artwork, small rugs, and lamps. If I could lift a particular piece of furniture, I'd be off and running with that, too.

Juxtapositions

One of the great joys of decorating is finding unlikely combinations that somehow flatter each other. Think smooth-rough, traditional-modern, shiny-dull, bright-plain, etc. Consider the possibilities:

- Pinecones in a glass bowl
- Folk art weather vane on a glass coffee table
- Chippendale high chest near an abstract painting
- Stark modern furniture with Audubon prints
- Buggy seat in front of a still-life painting
- Old geometric quilt in a contemporary setting

The appeal of this matte black vase *with raised ceramic leaves is heightened by its placement on a reflective glass coffee table created by Pennsylvania artisan John Zan. The glass reveals the unexpected underpinnings of old tools and hardware painted jet black. The decorative shell and whitish book jackets add brightness to the grouping.*

A lovely spring bouquet *fresh from the garden? No, it's a terrific fake! Today's realistically created silk and paper flowers add cheer to any room during bleak winter's bloomless days.*

- Want to maximize light? Look for unlined white paper styles, cut-and-punched paper styles, and light fabrics.

- Looking for a mood effect and more confined light? Consider black and darker paper shades for drama, fabric styles for charm, metal shades for their Colonial styles or a sleek high-tech look.

- Not every lamp comes with the most effective shade. Stand back and check a shade's color, proportions, and shape. A change of shade has the ability to transform a lamp and its place in a room. By changing to a different-size harp, it's possible to raise or lower the lampshade. A harp extender lifts the shade slightly.

If you don't have a terrific lighting store in your area, try the Brass Light Gallery of Milwaukee, Wisconsin (see Resources), for the stylish variety and quality of their lighting. There's

Many plants, *such as this jade plant, grow slowly, need a minimum of watering, and thrive in humidity. Used as a decorative accessory for a bathroom, they can warm up sleek hard surfaces with color and life.*

a charge for their complete catalog, but it's well worth the price of admission and is refundable with a purchase. Their lighting sampler overview is free.

A Quick Overview on Being Green

A potted tree is one of nature's accessories, and a place for eyes to rest in the depths of winter. But choosing the right type of indoor tree or potted plant becomes yet another design challenge, requiring you to consider shape, size, mass, and texture carefully.

Trailing grape ivy on a pedestal has the ability to fill an empty space gracefully. On the other hand, a giant philodendron in a small apartment can look as though it may have held the starring role in "The Plant That Ate Manhattan." Let's face the fact that certain plants are better suited to hotel lobbies.

If it's grace you're after, think of a ficus tree. For a bold statement, the elephant ear plant reaches out with fanlike leaves. I have a fondness for the stalwart corn plant, because it seems to grow for anyone and manages to do well under less-than-ideal conditions. Cactus plants come in many interesting shapes and varieties and are well suited to people who forget to water. Whether it's African violets or a palm tree, be sure that you match up the tree or plant with its various growing requirements.

Pillow Talk

Some people just can't get enough—they mix them, match them, fluff them, and go to extremes to find the perfect trimming. Even the bare-bones minimalist (two for the sofa and one for a good night's sleep) gives the accent pillow high marks. Pillows pull a room together, warm up a space, provide comfort, and introduce color, texture, and pattern. A sassy turquoise pillow becomes the color punch for a neutral piece; it's extra salsa to a hot color scheme. Softly colored florals bring thoughts of warm summer breezes to bleak winter days, while a scheme of all white (plenty of lace and ruffles) whispers of things Victorian.

The Pillow Sandwich

Think of an accent pillow as a textile sandwich—with a front, a back, and a filling. The creative combinations are endless. If you haven't yet discovered the joy of pillows as decorative accessories, we'll take a quick look at the basic forms, as well as the delicious menu for trimmings, also known by the French word *passementerie*.

Pillows fall into easy categories:

- Accent (also, throw or decorative)
- Bolster
- Floor cushion
- Novelty (from unusual shapes to sachets)

Name That Pillow!

Whether you're pillow shopping or working with a pillow-maker, it's important to be able to describe the style you have in mind. Following is a short glossary of pillow talk:

Box: The front and back are joined by a wide (from 1- to 3-inch) strip or border.

Knife edge: Front and back are joined with a single seam; this type has sharp corners.

Turkish: Borderless; corners are tucked into neat soft pleats.

Gathered: Similar to Turkish, but the corners are gathered.

Bolster: A roll, gathered or tailored at the ends.

Flange: A distinctive flat border, which is an extension of the pillow fabric ("self-border") or made with a contrasting fabric.

All Gussied Up

A more tailored room may need only fabulous raw-silk pillows, trimmed with the simplest cording; a formal setting may be more inviting with a generous play of pillows, trimmed to the hilt. Get creative and turn pillow design into an art.

Start thinking about the possibilities for decorative touches:

- Ruffles (from narrow and tight to wide and floppy)
- Antique lace or ruffled ribbons
- A decorative panel (from a circle of needlepoint sewn onto velvet to a square of organdy on linen)
- Appliqué (from Hawaiian quilt motifs to pictorial images)
- Ruching (when fabric is gathered tightly onto a thick filler cord)

Other ideas for decorative trimming include:

- Welting (a fabric-covered filler cord)
- Piping (a flat narrow fabric or braid trim)
- Corded piping (bias-cut fabric used over a filler cord)
- Cord (a decorative ropelike band, not to be confused with the functional filler cord)
- Fringe (from colorful ball fringe at one extreme to elegant tricolor silk fringe at the other)
- Tassels (from simple fabric ties at the corners to rich *passementerie*
- Braid
- Ribbons
- Buttons
- Bows
- Beading

Pillows Made Easy

In *Sewing Beautiful Pillows*, author Linda Lee applies many of the stylish techniques used in fine couture to pillows, giving them true character. Thanks to easy-to-follow instructions and many full-color photos for ideas, your passion for pillows need not cost a king's ransom.

Pillow Vision

You can create a great pillow from a priceless medieval tapestry or an old flour sack. It all depends on your vision for the pillow and for the room. With that said, there are certain fabrics that come to mind when thinking about appropriate textiles for pillows.

Think elegant: Needlework (needlepoint, crewel, embroidery), fragments from antique rugs, and cloths like linen, silk, velvet, and chintz.

Consider casual: Vintage florals, corduroy, chenille, sailcloth, and fragments from antique rugs, such as tribal and ethnic rugs.

Sense of country: Ticking, denims, quilting, fragments from timeworn textiles (hooked rugs, quilts, woven rugs, seat covers, tea towels).

Mostly modern: Leather, suede, glamorous synthetics (metalicized, chemically creased and textured).

Purely romantic: Linen, organdy, silk, lace, cotton florals, velvet, fragments from antique embroidered linens, wedding gowns, and vintage clothing.

Your Pillow's Inner Self

The meat in the pillow sandwich is known as the filler. Ready-made fillers come in a variety of pillow shapes and sizes, and are known as "pillow forms" or "pillow inserts."

■ The better synthetic fillers are a good choice for decorative pillows, especially for anyone allergic to feathers. Synthetic fillers come in different weights and qualities, and even the most expensive inserts are reasonably priced.

■ Duck or goose down combined with feathers is especially soft and comfortable, but double-check quality before you buy. Some mixes of feathers and down are too heavy on the feathers. Avoid feathers alone, which feel like cotton balls mixed with toothpicks.

■ My filler of choice is costly, but heavenly. One hundred percent goose down squashes into graceful folds, then springs right back with a quick shake. Although down compresses more quickly than synthetic fillers, a custom-made down pillow insert can be filled as solidly as a seat cushion or as light as a cloud. If you have the budget, think of fine down as a good investment.

■ No kapok or foam chips, please! They're lumpy and they don't hold up. The foam block has its uses for outdoor furniture, but is not always pleasing to the eye. Save the plastic-foam beads for the beanbag floor pillow.

Dealing in Down

When shopping for antiques, don't pass up a dreary old pillow. First, check to see if it's filled with wonderful old-fashioned down. You can make a new cover, and voilà, you've got an affordable down pillow. If you don't snap it up, the next pillow-maker will! Be sure to check the condition of old pillows for stains and odors. Minor signs of age can be cleaned away. But if the pillow feels damp or smells offensive, leave it.

A Useful Project: The Walkabout

Select a favorite decorative object in your home that's never managed to shine in its present display spot. Then take it on a Walkabout (see page 152).

Decorating Dilemmas

ADVICE FROM A WREATH-MAKER

Q: Someone gave me the most beautiful dried wreath and I'd like to keep it looking fresh for as long as possible. What care advice can you give me?

A: Kathy Baker, wreath designer and owner of Cube Mountain Products in New Hampshire, is in the best position to give advice. Kathy offers the following (and more) on her Web site, www.cubemtn.com:

■ Keep wreaths away from direct heat and out of direct sunlight. The light will fade the colors.

■ To remove dust, use a feather duster or a very soft brush.

■ Do not expose dried wreaths to weather. Rain and humidity will cause the flowers to droop and fade. Wreaths made with preserved flowers will do well in a protected location, such as on a porch door. Check with your source before putting any wreath outdoors.

■ With reasonable care, dried wreaths can stay looking fresh for at least two years.

RESOURCES

Great Catalogs and Their Web Sites

Catalog shopping has come a long way since Sears & Roebuck! Today, with the right catalogs at hand, or a computer hooked up to the Internet, it's possible to shop for every room of the house without leaving home. The resources selected for inclusion in *Home Nesting Basics* include popular and reliable sources. For the sake of convenience, the sources are listed by category.

TOTAL HOME FURNISHINGS

Ballard Designs
www.ballarddesigns.com
1-800-367-2775

Crate & Barrel
www.crateandbarrel.com
1-800-237-5672

Ethan Allen
www.ethanallen.com
1-800-228-9229

IKEA
www.ikea.com
1-800-434-4532

La-Z-Boy
www.lazyboy.com
1-734-241-2435

Martha by Mail
www.marthastewart.com
1-800-950-7130

Pottery Barn
www.potterybarn.com
1-888-779-5176

Restoration Hardware
www.restorationhardware.com
1-800-762-1005

West Elm
www.westelm.com
1-866-428-6468

Workbench
www.workbenchfurniture.com
1-877-243-5700

MOSTLY COUNTRY

Calico Corners
www.calico.com
1-800-213-6366

The Country House
www.thecountryhouse.com
1-800-331-3602

Crow's Nest Trading Co.
www.crowsnesttrading.com
1-800-900-8558

Eddie Bauer Home
www.eddiebauer.com
1-800-625-7935

Faith Mountain Company
www.faithmountain.com
1-540-987-8521

L.L. Bean Home
www.llbean.com
1-800-441-5713

Orvis Country Home
www.orvis.com
1-888-235-9763

Plow & Hearth
www.plowhearth.com
1-800-494-7544

Sturbridge Yankee Workshop
www.sturbridgeyankee.com
1-800-231-8060

MOSTLY TRADITIONAL

Gump's by Mail
www.gumps.com
1-800-882-8055

Horchow
www.horchow.com
1-877-944-9888

Monticello Gift Collection
www.monticello.org
1-800-243-1743

Scully & Scully
www.scullyandscully.com
1-800-223-3717

Williamsburg Marketplace
www.williamsburgmarketplace.com
1-800-414-6291

Winterthur
www.winterthurgifts.com
1-800-767-0500

REGIONAL FLAIR

Napa Style
www.napastyle.com
1-866-776-6272

Sundance
www.sundancecatalog.com
1-800-422-2770

FRENCH COUNTRY LIVING

Pierre Deux
www.pierredeux.com
1-800-774-3373

Rue de France
www.ruedefrance.com
1-800-777-0998

KITCHEN AND TABLETOP

Panache
www.panache.com
1-800-454-6587

Ross-Simons
www.rosssimons.com
1-800-835-0919

Sur la Table
www.surlatable.com
1-866-328-5412

Williams-Sonoma
www.williams-sonoma.com
1-877-812-6235

BED AND BATH

Bed Bath & Beyond
www.bedbathandbeyond.com
1-800-462-3966

Chambers
www.williams-sonomainc.com
1-800-334-9790

Coldwater Creek
www.coldwatercreek.com
1-800-510-2808

The Company Store
www.thecompanystore.com
1-800-323-8000

Cuddledown
www.cuddledown.com
1-800-323-6793

Garnet Hill
www.garnethill.com
1-800-870-3513

Horchow Fine Linen
www.horchow.com
1-877-944-9888

Linensource
www.linensource.com
1-800-434-9812

Pottery Barn Bed + Bath
www.potterybarn.com
1-800-779-5176

Schweitzer Linen
www.schweitzerlinen.com
1-800-554-6367

ART AND OBJECTS

Guild.com
www.guild.com
1-877-344-8453

Wisteria
www.wisteria.com
1-800-767-5490

LIBRARY MATTERS

Easton Press
www.eastonpress.com
1-800-367-4534

Levenger
www.levenger.com
1-800-544-0880

THE HOME OFFICE

Design Within Reach
www.dwr.com
1-800-944-2233

Lizell
www.lizell.com
1-800-718-8808

Reliable Home Office
www.reliablehomeoffice.com
1-800-869-6000

Staples
www.staples.com
1-800-378-2753

Viking Office Products
www.vikingop.com
1-800-711-4242

LAMPS AND LIGHTING

Shades of Light
www.shades-of-light.com
1-800-262-6612

RUGS AND FLOOR COVERING

Smith + Noble Rug Studio
www.smithandnoble.com
1-800-560-0027

Stark Carpet
www.dir-dd.com/stark-carpet-antiques.html/
1-212-752-9000

WINDOW TREATMENTS

Country Curtains
www.countrycurtains.com
1-800-876-6123

Great Windows
www.greatwindows.com
1-800-556-6632

Jane & Co.
www.janeandco.com
1-800-431-6550

Smith + Noble Windoware
www.smithandnoble.com
1-800-560-0027

STORAGE

Hold Everything
www.holdeverything.com
1-800-840-3596

FOR KIDS

Pottery Barn Kids
www.potterybarnkids.com
1-800-430-7373

THIS AND THAT

Exposures
www.exposuresonline.com
1-800-222-4947

Lillian Vernon
www.lillianvernon.com
1-800-545-5426

Signals
www.signals.com
1-800-806-8433

The Vermont Country Store
www.vermontcountrystore.com
1-802-362-8460

PORCH AND GARDEN

Charleston Gardens
www.charlestongardens.com
1-800-469-0118

Gardener's Eden
www.gardenerseden.com
1-800-822-9600

Gardener's Supply Company
www.gardeners.com
1-888-833-1412

Smith & Hawken
www.smith-hawken.com
1-800-940-1170

OUTDOOR FURNITURE

Frontgate
www.frontgate.com
1-800-626-6488

Hammacher Schlemmer
www.hammacher.com
1-800-321-1484

Walpole Woodworkers
www.walpolewoodworkers.com
1-800-343-6948

Wood Classics
www.woodclassics.com
1-845-255-7871

HOME PROJECTS

Brookstone Hardtofind Tools
www.brookstone.com
1-800-846-3000

Home Depot
www.homedepot.com
1-800-430-3376

House of Antique Hardware
www.houseofantiquehardware.com
1-888-223-2245

Improvements
www.improvementscatalog.com
1-800-985-6044

Lowe's Home Improvement Warehouse
www.lowes.com
1-800-890-5932

Renovator's Supply
www.rensup.com
1-800-659-2211

Rockler Woodworking Superstore

www.rockler.com

1-800-279-4441

CATALOGS WORTH THE CHARGE

The following companies charge a fee for their catalogs, often deducted from purchases. All can be found on-line as well.

Authentic Designs

www.authentic-designs.com

1-800-844-9416

Brass Light Gallery

(Charge applies to complete catalog only)

www.brasslight.com

1-800-243-9595

Judi Boisson American Home Collection

www.judiboisson.com

1-631-283-5466

Maine Cottage Furniture

www.mainecottage.com

1-207-846-1430

Woodard Weave

www.woodardweave.com

1-800-332-7847

Helpful Reading for the Home Decorator

If you'd like to expand on what you've learned in *Home Nesting Basics* or to find out more about a particular decorating matter, turn to the wide selection of useful books on the market. To kick off this bountiful list, here's a short list of books I've enjoyed.

BOOKS MENTIONED IN *HOME NESTING BASICS*:

American Hooked & Sewn Rugs: Folk Art Underfoot by Joel and Kate Kopp, University of New Mexico Press, 1995 (paperback).

Antiques Roadshow Primer by Carol Prisant, Workman Publishing, 1999 (paperback).

The Cheapskate Millionaire's Guide to Bargain Hunting in the Big Apple by Tracie Rozhon, Times Books, 1999 (paperback).

Color by Terry Trucco, PBC International, 1998.

The Decorating Book by Mary Gilliatt, Pantheon Books, 1987 (paperback).

Elegant and Easy Rooms by Dylan Landis, Dell Publishing, 1997 (paperback).

Formal Country by Pat Ross; illustrated by David Phelps, Friedman/Fairfax, 1999 (paperback).

Money Harmony by Olivia Mellan and Sherry Christie, Walker & Co., 2001.

The New Paint Magic by Jocasta Innes, Pantheon Books, 1992.

Oriental Carpets: A Complete Guide: The Classic Reference— Newly Updated & Revised by Murray L. Eiland and Murray Eiland III, Bullfinch Press, 2002.

Period Style by Mary Gilliatt, Little, Brown & Company, 1990.

Sewing Beautiful Pillows by Linda Lee, Sterling Publishing, 1998 (paperback).

Tile by Jill Herbers, Artisan Books, 2001 (paperback).

White by Design by Bo Niles, Stewart, Tabori & Chang, 1992 (paperback).

THE FOLLOWING TITLES MAY ALSO BE OF INTEREST:

Antiques Roadshow Collectibles by Carol Prisant, Workman Publishing, 2003.

Calico Corners Guide to Do-It-Yourself Decorating Wall Treatments by Jane Jessup, Funwood, Inc., 1974, revised 1980.

The Curtain Sketchbook 2 by Wendy Baker and Chrissie Carriere, Randall International, 1999 (paperback).

Decorating with Pictures by Stephanie Hoppen, Crown, 1998 (paperback).

The Encyclopedia of Window Fashions by Charles I. Randall and Patricia M. Howard, Randall International, 2002.

Home Decorating for Dummies by Patricia Hart McMillan and Katharine Kaye McMillan, IDG Books Worldwide, 1998 (paperback).

Room Redux: The Home Decorating Workbook by Joann Eckstut and Sheran James, Chronicle Books, 1999.

Acknowledgments

The backstage world of bookmaking involves countless professionals, who work against deadlines, computer glitches, and author error to produce fine books. In addition to thanking the core group of publishing people who made *Home Nesting Basics* possible, the most significant individuals being Joelle Delbourgo and Olga Vezeris, I'd like to acknowledge the photographers, artists, design experts, and home furnishing sources who made this book happen.

HOME FURNISHINGS

Page 48: Chandelier made of sheet metal (# 902) by Authentic Designs (see Resources, page 167).

Page 132: Bordered sisal rug from Smith + Noble Rug Studio (see Resources, page 166).

Page 143: Wood shutters from Smith + Noble Windoware (see Resources, page 166).

Pages 30, 37, 88, 107, 113, and 119: Furniture from Maine Cottage Furniture (see Resources, page 167). Also, chair on page 24, sofa and chair on page 74, and wicker table on page 102.

PICTURE CREDITS

All photographs have been printed with permission and are indicated by the page on which they appear in this book. Title page and chapter openings feature fabric designs from the Laura Ashley Country House Collection, the Laura Ashley Wovens By Color Collection (vols. 1 and 2), the Laura Ashley Classics Collection, and the Laura Ashley Children's Classics Collection, distributed exclusively by Kravet Fabrics. They have been adapted for use in *Home Nesting Basics* with permission of Kravet, Inc. Reference includes fabric pattern name, followed by colorway.

Isabelle - Vintage: 1; House Party - Berry: 5; Blackmoor - Primrose: 19; Gwyneth - Plum: 33; Nickerson - Butterscotch: 43; Brookside - Ebony: 59; Pinepoint - Celery: 69; Lilliput - Peony: 83; Wakeman - Chambray: 91; Lilabet - Berry: 105; Knollwood - Denim: 117; House Party - Plum: 129; Polyanthas - Vintage: 147; Overbrook - Leaf: 163

Photographs © Pat Ross: 9, 24, 36, 74, 76, 96, 102, 132, 150, 153, 156, 157.

Taken from *Formal Country* by Pat Ross, all photographs © 1989 by David Phelps: 11 (top left and right), 46, 79, 86, 98, 138, 151.

Reprinted with permission of David Phelps Photography © David Phelps: 11 (bottom), 93

Photograph by Max Pine, courtesy Max Pine: 13

Photographs by Dennis Welsh. Reprinted with permission of Maine Cottage Furniture: 30, 37, 88, 107, 113, 119

Reprinted with permission of Authentic Designs: 48

Photograph by Brad Stephens, courtesy Brad Stephens: 124

Photograph by Eugene Kienzle: 131

Reprinted with permission of Smith + Noble, LLC: 143

Index